The Call of the Cascadura

A memoir

By

Michael De Gale

...so, my progeny may know from whence they came.

Dedicated to ...

Gabrielle, Stefan, Saniya and Mihaela

May your lives abound with prosperity, integrity, and
notable intellectual accomplishments,
rendering you, invaluable assets to humanity,
that can neither be bought nor sold.

In honor of...

The resilient spirits of our ancestors, whose enduring courage amidst epochs of adversity has fortified their progeny with the resolve to persevere, unwavering, until the resounding echoes of triumph fill the air.

Acknowledgements

I extend my heartfelt appreciation to my friends and family for their unwavering love and support throughout the process of writing this book. I am particularly grateful to my dear friend and confidant, Mary K, whose steadfast belief in my capabilities and consistent encouragement have been indispensable.

Copyright © Michael De Gale, 2022

All Rights Reserved

It is not legal to reproduce, duplicate, or transmit any part of this book in either electronic means or printed format. Recording of this publication is strictly prohibited.

Table of Contents

A Bird's Eye View	7
The Abyss	13
In a Land of Milk and Honey	21
The Conversation	24
The Unexplored Path	27
The Process of Transition	30
A Gift of Warmth	35
Nature's Wrath	41
Destination Bound	46
Welcome to Winnipeg	51
The Stage Beckons	73
Winter Weather	85
Reflections	91
Drama on the High Sea	109
Growing Up on The Island	113
Adventures and Tragedies	120
Remembering Meg	129
The Price of Admission	135
Making my Way	144
Family Relations	156
The Reunion	162
Toronto Bound	165
A Fractured Foundation	169
The World's Smallest Bookstore	175
A Shocking Revelation	193
Published Articles	215
Conclusion	305

A Bird's Eye View

The Boeing 747 soared gracefully into the blue Caribbean sky, often portrayed on postcards and the glossy pages of travel magazines, enticing the tired and the weather weary with regenerative promises of sun, sea water and sand. Against this backdrop of nature's flawless tapestry, a solitary hawk hovered high above a flock of native birds, gliding effortlessly on the currents of a gentle breeze. Oblivious to the impending threat, the birds remained in formation, casually executing the mechanics of flight, while basking in the ecstasy of unrestricted freedom. As fragments of marshmallow clouds drifted slowly towards the horizon, the thunderous sound of the passing aircraft did nothing to ruffle the feathers of these graceful creatures. Like their streetwise cousins in the presence of oncoming traffic, they casually dispersed, then quietly re-established their dominance of the air space in which they were clearly lord and master. The birds' apparent indifference to this intrusion seemed carefully rehearsed, attaining an unparalleled level of perfection, refined by the passage of time. Although I had witnessed this remarkable display of avian aeronautics on numerous occasions, I was captivated by the grace with which they accommodated their aluminum guest, signifying by their calm demeanor, that this was an intrusion to which they had long grown accustomed. However, the sudden appearance of an alien object in their celestial environment was the least of their concerns, for as they returned to formation, the sharp-eyed villainous hawk continued to hover, still waiting for an opportunity to strike.

Observing this fascinating interplay between nature and machine, I couldn't help but reflect on the fleeting nature of such encounters, knowing that the bustling metropolis awaiting my arrival may never afford me the privilege of ever witnessing such unblemished beauty again.

Nestled snugly between a rotund traveller and a window on the aircraft, I viewed with sacred adoration the fertile landscape unfolding beneath me, its meandering roads and tranquil rivers cutting deep into the belly of the island, so warm, so fertile, so green. Across this rolling terrain extending as far as the eye could see, lush green fields and widely scattered houses dotted the natural landscape in hues of reds and pinks and blues. In fields of avocado green where dairy cows grazed listlessly, flicking their tails at random to swat away bothersome flies that hastily disperse, only to return with increasing aggravation.

Like a colossus standing tall in the distance, a majestic mountain range rose exultingly towards the heavens, its emerald, green slopes, shielding the island from hurricane wind while amplifying its natural beauty. A geological spectacle and extension of the Andes Mountains, the Northern Range cradles the island's coastline in a protective embrace. From the Chaguaramas Peninsula in the west to the tranquil fishing village of Toco in the east, its rugged contours merging seamlessly with the blue waters of the Caribbean Sea. In the month of May, when Poui trees burst into a symphony of blooms, this mountain transforms into a breathtaking canopy of canary yellow. As if possessed by the spirit of an ancestral dancer, its rolling slopes sways effortlessly to the rhythm of the tropical breeze. This wave-like dance performance is the island's farewell gesture to those who must leave its warm waters and sunbathed shores. An invitation to return to a place where beauty flourishes, and natural resources are multiple and abundant.

Yet, beyond these picturesque landscapes lies a tapestry woven with the rich threads of conquest and resistance, culture, and heritage. Like a beacon shining brightly through a dark past Trinidad and Tobago, a tiny twin island nation, has left an indelible mark on the global stage in every endeavour, not the least of which is arts and culture. From the pulsating rhythms of calypso to the luminous hues of its carnival celebration, the island's cultural tapestry reflects a legacy of creativity and ingenuity.

Through the indigenous artistry of calypso, the esteemed Mighty Sniper memorialized the essence of the island in his masterwork *"Portrait of Trinidad"*, skillfully painting with words, a vivid image of its beauty and opulence. With his lyrical mastery, he conjured visions of a realm reminiscent of King Solomon's fabled mines, teeming with the treasures of nature and cultural abundance. Similarly, Allister Macmillan's verses in the monumental poem "Trinidad: Iere, Land of the Hummingbird" eloquently captured the fascinating essence of Trinidad, intertwining the legend of the Cascadura to craft a mesmerizing narrative of enchantment and awe.

He wrote,

Those who eat the cascadura will, the native legend says,

Wheresoever they may wander, end in Trinidad their days.
And this lovely fragrant island, with its forest hills sublime,
Well might be the smiling Eden pictured in the Book divine.
Cocoa woods with scarlet glory of the stately Immortelles,
Waterfalls and fertile valleys, precipices, fairy dells,
Rills and rivers, green savannahs, fruits and flowers and odours rich,
Waving sugar cane plantations and the wondrous lake of pitch.
Oh! the Bocas at the daybreak—how can one describe that scene!
Or the little emerald islands with the sapphire sea between!
Matchless country of Iere, fairer none could ever wish.
Can you wonder at the legend of the cascadura fish?

The mesmerizing beauty of which Macmillan speaks, convinces him that those who eat the Cascadura shall find their way back home, regardless of where they may wander. As I commenced my voyage towards the great white north without a predetermined date of return, I found myself wondering whether this mystical island might one day become my final resting place as this native lore foretold.

Gazing upon the verdant landscape unfolding below, I could not help but marvel at the profound beauty of this island. From its sun-kissed shores to its vibrant cultural heritage, Trinidad and Tobago stands as a testament to the enduring spirit of resilience and creativity that defines its people. Like the pitch lake flung far in the southwest corner of the island, it displays a casual beauty that bubbles up from the belly of the people, the music in their laughter, the tempo in the way they speak, and the pulsating rhythm of steel pan music and calypso, poignant reminders to its restless children, that this enchanted island will always be home.

As the aircraft maintained its trajectory through the sapphire sky, a vast expanse of water that mirrored the heavens above, came sharply into focus. Its glistening surface strewn with fishing boats in a kaleidoscope of colours, bobbing on the rolling waves like jetsam from a recent shipwreck. Upon the undulating crests of the waves, dolphins maintained a precarious balance, swiftly retreating before the tumultuous waves crash upon the shore where the mountain stood tall on one side, and coconut trees lined the sandy beach, like sentinels on the other.

On the gleaming sand where exuberant children frolicked with delight, a bubbling caldron sat in the flames of a roaring fire, releasing tendrils of smoke and steam deep into the atmosphere. Like a mystical presence hovering lazily above the land, the aromatic essence of a timeless stew infused with spices permeated the air, conjuring mouth-watering memories of curried crabs and dumplings, evoking an insatiable longing for its flavorful embrace. In the deepest recesses of my mind, a hot red pepper erupted in the pot, releasing the tantalizing aroma of distant memories that left me yearning for one more taste of that delightful concoction.

Further in the distant where sky and sea merged seamlessly, a vessel rested precariously on the edge of the ocean as if frozen in time. Against this boundless backdrop of sun and sea, it struck me as a work of art, adorned in shades of azure, slate, and ivory. Although I had beheld the grandeur of this island and the expansive sea that surrounds it on several occasions, only marginally did it ever register on the periphery of my conscious mind. Yet now, it unfolded before me with the wonderment of a child encountering the world for the very first time.

As I struggled to etch these fleeting impressions onto the canvas of my mind, the aircraft became engulfed in a dense cloud, completely obscuring the land that had rocked me gently in my cradle. Wrapped loosely within this vaporous realm, I pondered the existence of the stirring images that had seized my senses, questioning whether they were tangible realities or merely figments of my highly stimulated imagination.

"Was McMillan correct?" I wondered. "Could this truly be the fabled Garden of Eden envisioned in the sacred text as McMillian has stated?"

For more than just a fleeting moment, a deep conviction and national pride surged from deep within, convincing me of the island's authenticity.

The Abyss

While enveloped in a blanket of clouds, soft and white as a bed of cotton, an intense silence filled the empty space. In this vaporous enclosure, punctuated by the persistent hum of the engine and the serving of sustenance, I found myself in a state of solitude. Hungry and weary, I dined voraciously, until the weight of excess began to weigh upon me. Despite the fatigue relentlessly tugging at my eyelids, I resisted the urge to succumb to slumber, only to find myself drifting into a threshold state, wedged precariously between consciousness and dreams. Suddenly, I experienced an alarming sensation where the seat gave way beneath me, hurtling me into a void darker than the depths of night. Amidst the freefall, I heard my screams echoing into the abyss before the fall abruptly halted, leaving me suspended in darkness like an apostrophe to fear, gripped by an intense melancholy. Unable to comprehend the terror that had enveloped me, I surrendered my petrified, black body to the unknown fate that awaited.

Alone in this abyss, devoid of earthly markers, reality blurred with the realm of imagination. There was no way of knowing how much time had passed, neither could I distinguish between what was real, from that which was imagined. Through the darkness, I sought solace in the reassurance that what I was experiencing was but a dream, albeit one more harrowing than any psychological thriller that had ever been produced.

Deep in the bowels of unfathomable darkness, I could neither see myself nor the hand that I held up before me. Teleported to an alternate universe, stripped of my physical being and existing only in a state of compromised consciousness, I was convinced that I had descended into hell.

Yet, no demon, inferno, or disembodied voices addressed me—only a profound silence. With no bearings, I questioned my very sanity, my existence enveloped in eternal obscurity. Afraid that I had lost my mind, I shouted through the darkness.

"Is this Limbo?"

"Is this Purgatory?"

"Am I in hell?"

"Is anyone there?"

Except for the sound of my own voice penetrating deep into the darkness, nothing was heard, but a deafening silence.

Grappling with the inexplicable, I searched my conscience for any transgressions deserving of the fate that had befallen me. Finding none, I confronted the possibility of divine retribution for my disbelief in the existence of God. Consumed by fear, I envisioned a vengeful God raining fire and brimstone upon me and the lake of fire in which I would burn for all eternity. In desperation, I pleaded for forgiveness, only to be met by the chilling realization of my eternal condemnation. If only to confirm my sanity, a response from a disembodied voice would have been welcomed, but I heard nothing. Contemplating the justice of my plight, I pondered the fate of those who had perpetrated heinous crimes against humanity. If the wages for my sins warranted eternal darkness, what then of those who had committed atrocities of unparalleled magnitude?

I reflected upon the destiny of Adolph Hitler, Mussolini, and King Leopold of Belgum, who orchestrated the systematic slaughter, dismemberment, and subjugation of millions in the Congo. Likewise, I questioned the ultimate outcome for those who perpetrated the barbaric enslavement of countless Africans, forcibly uprooting them from their homes and subjecting them to centuries of bondage.

As I delved into these reflections, I could not help but wonder if divine justice awaited these perpetrators, as scripture suggests. If I am to endure eternal darkness for my sins, then surely there must be proportionate retribution for those who inflicted such profound suffering upon the Bakongo people of the Congo and Angola, the Mandé of Upper Guinea, the Gbe speakers of Togo and Benin, the Akan of Ghana and the Ivory Coast, the Wolof of Senegal and the Gambia, and countless others whose names were never recorded. If banishment into eternal darkness is the price I must pay, then they are surely being consumed by the eternal fires of Hell.

While reflecting on the fate of those who perpetrated egregious crimes against humanity, the resounding echoes of African drums permeated the darkness. I heard the Djembe, the Dundun, the Bata, the Bougarabou, the Tamanin, the Lunna, and the Kalangu—talking drums of Africa—summoning lost souls with a rhythm that was mournful and profound. The thunderous soul-searching sound enveloped the darkness, growing louder and louder until I could no longer resist its power. Overcome by its overwhelming embrace, my heart surrendered to the rhythm of the talking drums.

Then slowly, from the depths of the darkness distorted images emerged, unleashing a torrent of emotions. Millions of men, women, and children, were being viciously torn from their homes in Africa, chained together, and forced to embark on harrowing journeys overland. Overcome by exhaustion and despair after months of travel, millions perished along the route, their emaciated bodies discarded with indifference and indignity.

For more than three hundred years, the seas bore witness to unspeakable horrors as ships from England, Spain, Portugal, France, and other European nations, traversed their depths laden with the baneful site of human cargo. Year after year, they made these sordid journeys, their putrid bowels crammed beyond capacity with the sons and daughters of Africa dying in vomit, blood, and human shit. In the bellies of these demonic ships, diseases spread like wildfire killing millions more along the Middle Passage. Fearing the unknown, many leaped and others were thrown overboard, as creatures emerged from the depts of the ocean, to frantically feed on human flesh. For hundreds of years, the waters of the Atlantic churned vigorously with the blood of Africa's sons and daughters. A grim testament to the inhumanity of the transatlantic slave trade and those who perpetrated this heinous crime against humanity.

Being savagely torn from Africa however, marked only the beginning of their tribulation. In what Europeans called the "New World", Africans were paraded like livestock on auction blocks and sold to the highest bidder, while curious crowds gathered to delight in human suffering.

Yet, in the presence of unceasing brutality, these remarkable people clung tenaciously to live, enduring an unparallel level of suffering that would have annihilated a less resilience race.

In waving fields of sugar cane and crimson blood, stripped of their humanity and the soothing balm of love, unspeakable cruelties occurred, perpetrated by demons masquerading in human form. In these fields I saw their tortured faces and the flow of African blood that fertilized the plantations in which sugarcane was grown to fuel the economies of Europe. In these bitter fields of pain and bondage, the Third Estate of color was born. Among the multitude were my ancestors, enslaved on sugar cane plantations and subjected to the depravities of an alien race, relentless in their pursuit of crown and title. My senses recoiled as twisted whips cut deep into dark flesh, while they toiled and perished under the lash and the weight of labor. Unable to bear the unfolding savagery, I averted my gaze, yet the chorus of agony persisted unabated. Then, like a bridge linking the present to the past, random images alternated between joy and sorrow, pleasure, and pain. I saw myself in childhood, my mother, my father, my brothers, my sisters, my friends of long ago, the progeny of a proud people who gave civilization to the world. Events, once hidden in the deepest recesses of my soul erupted like a volcano, spewing vivid images across the open sky. Then as slowly as it began, the images quietly faded, leaving me to ponder the savagery that was laid before me.

For the ancestors who suffered mercilessly, sugar cane was never sweet. Yet, despite the tyranny they endured at the hands of those who sought to exploit their labor, their resilience amidst brutality forged a legacy of strength, enabling the descendants of these resilient souls to emerge, reclaim our narrative and assert our rightful place in world history.

In the solitude of darkness, I finally grasp the profound significance of my presence in this alternate universe. I was there to bear witness to the greatest atrocity that had ever been perpetrated against a people in the history of humanity. Overwhelmed and fatigued, I felt a nervous urge to laugh, but there was no sound. Instead, my eyes clouded over, and tears—four centuries in the making—streamed down like the rain that keeps the island green and provides moisture where the sugarcane still grows. Amidst unfathomable cruelty, the descendants of Africans asserted their humanity, creating an ethnically diverse Utopia for me and over one million of my kin and countrymen. Buried deep in their resilient seeds were the promise of a future where our voices will continue to echo the struggles and triumphs of our ancestors' as we forge a way forward.

Emerging from a lingering haze of compromised consciousness, my mind wandered to the island – its rich history, vibrant culture, and resilient people. In my travels near and far, the island never faded from my thoughts. Like the unwavering love of a mother, I took its presence for granted, always confident it would welcome me back with open arms. Each return brought a rush of emotion as the familiar sight of the mountain greeted me. My heart would leap as the mountain came into view, its peak reaching high above the land as if to welcome home its prodigal son.

Growing up from man-child to man on the landscape of this enchanting island, I savored both its joys and sorrows. Here, I sowed seeds of prosperity on land and in woman, yielding fruits with an ebony hue and of exquisite quality. My roots dug deep into the island's soil, inextricably binding me to it. Though my navel string was not ceremoniously buried under a banana tree as tradition dictated, this island was the only home that I had ever truly known.

The final departure and impending separation weighed heavily on my heart as I recalled the legend of the Cascadura, a poem about the freshwater catfish that travels over land to immerse itself in the muddy bottoms of slow-moving rivers, drainage ditches, and swamps. Despite its questionable choice of habitat, the Cascadura is rumoured to be a culinary delight when curried with coconut milk, hot peppers, and onions, served on a bed of rice. Forced under the threat of lash, to commit this poem to memory, its significance had faded over time. Yet now, faced with the prospect of permanent departure, its warning echoed loudly in my mind.

Despite my frequent travels, the notion of leaving permanently had never been at issue until now. But as the poem's prophecy lingered, conscious that I have never tasted one morsel of this fish so deeply entrenched in the island's mythology, I pondered the possibility that my neglect of the revered Cascadura might seal my fate, forever alienating me from my beloved island.

In a Land of Milk and Honey

The chance to emigrate had never crossed my path before, nor did I harbor any strong inclination to relocate to a land promising abundance. My upbringing was nestled on this lush island, where the morning sun would spread its golden light across the land, and a beach was never far away. If there was milk and honey to be found anywhere, it would be here, in this Caribbean haven. To stake my claim to its riches, I joined a group of Insurance Brokers—regular folks who, through grit and determination, had lifted themselves up from the bonds of deprivation. They believed that success, much like beauty, is subjective and should be flaunted.

Their mantra was simple: "Fake it till you make it."

Fueled by ambition and a fervent desire to carve out my part from this land of plenty, what initially seemed like a distant dream soon solidified into reality. In a relatively short span, I acquired plenty—a sleek vehicle, tailored suits, investments in the stock market, and a condominium in the gated community of Flagstaff Hill. This stunning new enclave nestled at the foothills of Maraval, where every morning, the cool mountain air left a thin veneer of mist that blanketed the area. To ensure safety, particularly for its residents comprising doctors, lawyers, engineers, and other professionals, security personnel manned the entrance day and night. Its proximity to the city center, affordability, and access to amenities made it an ideal choice. Moreover, being adjacent to the American Ambassador's residence was an added security bonus. Reflecting on it even then, the ambiance of this area stood in stark contrast to the economically depressed community where I had spent a substantial amount of my formative years. The simple appearance of success garnered trust from clients who readily entrusted their affairs to me and the organization I represented. I became recognizable on the streets of Port of Spain, greeted with nods of approval, or so it seemed. Despite my burgeoning ideological leanings towards the left that contrasted sharply with the mindset of my mentors, I was well on my way to becoming a Black bourgeoisie. Admittedly, my political acumen was still in a embryonic stage when I ventured into the insurance realm. Nonetheless, the allure of unlimited earning potential was difficult to ignore, especially with a young family to support. Having already tasted the sweet nectar of success, I knew its sweetness would only intensify with time. To me, every potential client was a diamond in the rough—ripe for discovery, refinement, and brilliance. They were everywhere, raw, uncut, acres of diamonds. With a stroke of my pen, I secured financial stability for clients and their loved ones in the event of disability or untimely death. Over the years, my counsel had proven invaluable for my clients while simultaneously paving the way for my own prosperity.

However, conventional wisdom warns that unlike disappointment, opportunities knock infrequently, and failing to seize them may lead to a lifetime of regret. In Shakespeare's Twelfth Night, Malvolio famously proclaimed,

"Some are born great, some achieve greatness, and some have greatness thrust upon them."

While my story isn't one of greatness, I was meticulously mining to my "acres of diamonds" when the unexpected opportunity to immigrate presented itself. Recognizing that such opportunities are rare, I decided to embrace it. With two young children whose future hinged on my choices, it was prudent to explore this offer.

The Conversation

The tale unfurled back in the summer haze of 1987, when my wife's uncle and his spouse sought solace on our sun-kissed island from the everyday grind of life in Canada. Years had elapsed since his last visit, and the allure of reconnecting with the old country beckoned him, alongside his Irish wife, eager for the adventure. Amidst beach jaunts and explorations of historical sights, they stumbled upon Smoky and Bunty, a local watering hole renowned for its lively ambiance. Here, the vibrant beats of soca and calypso music set a festive tone that persisted from dawn till dusk. To ease the intoxicating effects of Carib lager and Stag beer, they indulged in a medley of culinary delights ranging from rotis to Chinese food. For Phyllis, the dark, robust taste of Guinness Extra Stout stirred nostalgic memories of her homeland, while the island's cuisine tantalized her taste buds like never before. Enveloped in the jubilant atmosphere and basking under the tropical sun, she declared that Trinidad is the closest she had even been to paradise.

In the backdrop of Winnipeg, Phyllis thrived as an Insurance Broker affiliated with Mutual of Omaha, renowned for its sponsorship of the acclaimed "Wild Kingdom". This long-running television documentary series featured wildlife and nature though not without controversy. Over dinner, we traded tales of our successes in the insurance realm, both recipients of accolades and poised to grace another sales convention.

"If you were selling insurance in Winnipeg," she mused, "your success would surpass all expectations."

Though her words were pleasing, I couldn't help but chuckle. Winnipeg, in my mind, seemed a far cry from success, a land too cold for folks of our hue. Yet, we toyed with the notion of immigration, engaging in speculative discourse. As they bid farewell and flew back to Canada, I returned to my endeavors, meticulously mining my own treasures.

Immigrating had never occupied my mind until Phyllis planted the seed that somehow fell on fertile soil and quickly began to take root. Despite years of dedicated labor, I found myself pondering why her suggestion resonated. Was it the relentless competition? The desire for new horizons? Or perhaps, the allure of a bigger world beyond our shores? She mentioned that Winnipeg has a relatively large Black population. Maybe she thought that I could tap into that lucrative demographic for our mutual benefit. We both knew how difficult it is to recruit a sales force that is ethical, committed and highly effective. Perhaps that was the reason she dangled the bait before me. As weeks turned into months, her proposition faded into the backdrop of my daily routine. Yet, when sponsorship documents eventually arrived a few months later, excitement mingled with apprehension.

Contemplating the implications of immigration, I grappled with the vision of my own insurance brokerage versus the prospects for my children in a bustling metropolis.

"Is it worth exploring?" I mused.

After days of internal debate, I found myself at a crossroads, uncertain of the path ahead. If my application was declined, there would be no love lost, and my dream of managing my own brokerage firm on the island could still be realized. Alternatively, if it was approved, should I defer my dream to go tilting at windmills as Don Quixote had done? Those were questions that could neither be easily dismissed, nor could they be taken lightly.

Ultimately, I chose to submit the documents to the Canadian Embassy, recognizing that whether accepted or declined, the journey ahead held significant implications for my dreams and aspirations.

The Unexplored Path

Throughout my adult life, I have adhered to the conventional routes, competently navigating the complexities that unfolded along the familiar journey. The prospect of immigrating to Canada ignited a distinct curiosity, offering a path I had yet to traverse. Nonetheless, I hesitated to forsake the strides I had already made. As the adage goes,
"a bird in the hand is worth two in the bush."
While I hold profound respect for wisdom, it's undeniable that elders can sometimes offer misguided counsel. With significant considerations at play, I resolved to personally explore the opportunities that awaited me in the City of Winnipeg.
In the summer of 1988, I embarked on an exploratory trip to Winnipeg, and was immediately struck by the city's cleanliness. Contrastingly, the streets of my hometown, were often strewn with refuse, a regrettable norm that had long been rooted in the local landscape. Winnipeg, however, boasted strategically placed waste bins, promoting responsible disposal practices. The bins were easy on the eyes, and if a garbage container was not immediately available, people would hold on to their trash until it was convenient to dispose of it. To do otherwise would stir one's conscience but more importantly, the consequences would be severe. Non-compliance was met with stringent enforcement of municipal bylaws and substantial fines, ensuring the city's pristine appearance.

The city's infrastructure catered to pedestrian comfort, with benches dotting its landscape, providing spaces for relaxation and contemplation amidst the urban hustle. Moreover, vibrant floral displays adorned the cityscape, transforming Winnipeg into a veritable urban garden. Maintenance crews diligently tended to green spaces, ensuring their aesthetic appeal remained intact. In open areas, people played with dogs that showed no signs of exhaustion, regardless of how many times they were ordered to fetch. Parks bustled with activity, as residents soaked in the sun and engaged in recreational pursuits. On bustling restaurant patios packed to capacity, patrons savored culinary delights and intoxicating beverages, topped with cherries and umbrellas to add an air of sophistication. In the warmth of the summer heat, they paraded in tee shirts, shorts, and sandals. It was clear that summer was a special time of year that people embraced with gusto and reverence; a phenomenon that struck me as peculiar.

While my upbringing in a tropical climate had conditioned me to avoid excessive sun exposure, by contrast, Winnipeggers embraced the summer months with fervor, indulging in outdoor activities with unwavering enthusiasm that I found difficult to comprehend. In time, I too would come to embrace summer and the routine indulgences that made it a spectacle in the eyes of the uninitiated.

In my homeland, music serves as the lifeblood of cultural expression, a ubiquitous presence in daily life. However, in Winnipeg, the diverse cultural tapestry necessitated a mutual respect for individual preferences, fostering harmony amidst varying musical tastes. Throughout the length of my stay, I met people from all walks of life who made me feel welcomed and respected. On learning of the reason for my visit, many encouraged me to stay.

The prevalence of interracial families and the affordability of essential amenities underscored Winnipeg's commitment to inclusivity and socio-economic accessibility. Although unaware of the historical injustices endured by Indigenous communities, my initial interactions affirmed the city's reputation for human warmth and hospitality, giving credence to its motto, "Friendly Manitoba," a fitting moniker and a testament to the benefits of cultural diversity.

By the conclusion of my exploratory visit, I harbored a growing affinity for Winnipeg, envisioning it as my potential new home. I understood that it would take time to become accustomed to the unpainted buildings and the deafening sound of silence. There were no houses painted in all the colors of the rainbow. The soca and calypso music that breathes life into the island would not be routinely heard on city streets, and the food that had sustained me for so long would not be as readily accessible. Despite the inevitable challenges of cultural adjustment, I remained captivated by the city's allure. Two weeks later, armed with empirical insights, I returned home, awaiting the verdict of Canadian immigration authorities. Several months thereafter, my immigration documents arrived, bearing the seal of approval, affirming my decision to embark on this uncharted journey.

The Process of Transition

With the conclusion of my immigration paperwork and the establishment of a confirmed departure date, a period of strategic restructuring ensued. Over the succeeding weeks, I bid farewell to acquaintances and loved ones, navigating a spectrum of emotions. Anticipating a vigorous resistance from my agency manager, I deliberately withheld the news of my imminent departure until all other farewells had been exchanged. Recognizing the necessity to alleviate financial strain on my spouse, I embarked on the task of liquidating assets. Foremost among these was the sale of my 1986 Nissan Laurel, a once-luxurious vehicle that had recently sustained damage to its windshield. Conscious of my impending relocation, I opted against replacing the windshield, willing to accept a loss in its sale. Shortly after posting an advertisement, the vehicle was sold at a value commensurate with its original purchase price from just two years prior, when I drove it off the lot as a brand-new vehicle. Relinquishing possession of my condominium, I later learned of its appreciable market valuation, regretting my decision to forego its potential return. After finally liquidating various other assets, my spouse was better equipped to manage our financial affairs in my absence.

Mr. T, my agency manager and mentor, was a highly skilled sales professional who would leave no stone unturned to persuade me to reconsider my decision. He was a towering black man, six feet three inches tall, with a slim build and a thick mustache. Always impeccably dressed, he looked as if he had just stepped from the pages of GQ Magazine. His

Mercedes Benz, gold Rolex watch, and the diamond ring that he regularly sported on his pinkie finger, were visual symbols of his remarkable success. In all the years that I had known Mr. T, I had never seen him without a suit, and couldn't imagine him otherwise. Suits were our uniform, and not being impeccably attired was unthinkable. He would often compliment us on our dress and would take the time to straighten our ties if needed. How we were perceived by the public was of the utmost importance to him and he never ceased to remind us to look professional, evenings and weekends posed no exception. The job of an Insurance Broker is not a nine to five, he often said, and never hesitated to lead by example. As the date of my departure drew closer, I scheduled an appointment to meet with him in private.

Engaging in a private audience with Mr. T, marked a pivotal moment as my departure neared. The gravity of my forthcoming revelation permeated the atmosphere, usually characterized by customary pleasantries and casual discourse. Recognizing his typically composed demeanor wane in response to the unexpected privacy of our meeting, I delicately broached the subject of my departure due to the impending impact and implications of my decision. Despite our longstanding professional rapport, I remained resolute in my resolve, prepared for the ensuing dialogue.

"What's up?" He asked, getting directly to the reason for our unconventional meeting.

I paused for a moment, leaving the question to marinate until a discomforting silence ensued. Whenever Mr. T was stressed, he would tighten his jaw, which contradicted his attempt to appear composed.

"Well, wah yuh want to talk bout?" He inquired again.

Still contemplating his likely response, I hesitated a bit longer.

"Wah's de problem? He asked again with increasing urgency.

"Ah leaving the agency," I said.

The words exploded like a bomb in his head.

"Wah!" he exclaimed, almost falling off his chair.

He was clearly not prepared for the news that I had broken. Genuinely surprised, he began by confirming what I had clearly announced.

"Wah yuh say, yuh say yuh leaving the agency?"

"Yeah," I replied. "Ah moving to Canada."

Mr. T. and I had developed an excellent working relationship over a period of several years, and I knew that my departure would come as a shock to him. Since joining the agency, I have learned a lot from him about the psychology of sales. Training courses, instinct, seminars, and the many sales conventions I had attended over the years had transformed me into a veritable sales professional. Since he too was highly skilled, I figured that his first approach would involve logic and common sense. If that failed, I expected him to appeal to my emotions.

"Yuh serious?" he asked incredulously.

"Yeah," I said. "Ah serious, ah moving to Winnipeg."

"You must be crazy." He responded.

Seemingly puzzled, he inquired,

"Why you go give up all yuh done accomplish to start again from scratch, not to mention the promising future yuh have here?"

I thanked him for his concern and apologized for the inconvenience that my departure was sure to have on the agency.

"Yuh making ah big mistake." He assured me.

Then his story telling skills as a gifted sales professional slipped into high gear. He reminded me of how he had left the Trinidad Police Force to become an insurance broker and within a few years, he presided over his own agency with more than twenty brokers and was still growing. He declared that, based on my track record, he had no doubt that I would have my own brokerage firm one day. He mentioned other colleagues in the business who had risen through the ranks and of the lifestyle that they were enjoying. We spoke for over an hour, and although I was acutely aware of all that he had said, I was still unmoved. Understandably, he was upset and with good reason. I was one of his star brokers, and my departure was certain to have a negative impact on the agency's bottom line. This was further exacerbated by the fact that another high-performing broker was also leaving the agency to go abroad. In a desperate attempt to dissuade me from leaving, he talked about the ups and downs of immigrating and although the merits of his argument were substantive, it all fell on deaf ears. All that he had said was true, but I remained steadfast, determined not to change my mind. Considering my determination to leave, his demeanor changed, and he was now visibly upset. As a last resort, I thought he would play the guilt card, although that would have been out of character and would have reeked of desperation. I had a great deal of respect for this man who was my role model and I hoped that he would not lower himself to speak of how much he had done for me. Granted that I was a novice when I first joined the agency, and he had done much to improve my selling skills, without my determination to succeed and gift of gab, it would have all added up to naught. Over a period of several years, we had both seen this unfold time and again, where seemingly ambitious young men and women joined the organization, received the necessary training but couldn't cut it in the field. To his credit, he never went there.

Over the course of our discussion, Mr. T unleashed an arsenal of logic, emotion, and personal anecdotes, appealing to my sensibilities but to no avail. Remaining steadfast in my determination, I expressed gratitude for his mentorship while reaffirming my commitment to pursuing opportunities abroad. While acknowledging the potential ramifications of my departure on the organization, I resolved to prioritize the welfare of my family above all else.

In the aftermath of our exchange, I departed with a renewed sense of purpose, cognizant of the challenges ahead yet steadfast in my conviction. While Mr. T's sentiments were noted, my unwavering commitment to my family's future remained unyielding.

A Gift of Warmth

Immediately preceding my departure, in keeping with the warm hospitality characteristic of West Indian culture, my friend Vincent paid an unexpected visit. Before I could extend a formal invitation to enter, he had already made himself at home in my living room. Vincent, a slender figure with small, enigmatic eyes set deeply within the contours of his narrow face, belied an unassuming disposition despite his sketchy outward appearance. Beneath the surface, he was a person of integrity, grappling with the same human vulnerabilities shared by all.

" Whappening, boy?" he greeted me, his smile reminiscent of the enigmatic Cheshire Cat from Lewis Carroll's literary classic, "Alice in Wonderland."

" Ah hear yuh leaving we, so ah come to see yuh before yuh go," he continued.

" Ah didn't expect to see you here," I responded.

" Whappening with you?" I inquired.

Although Vincent's initial inquiry seemed casual, it betrayed a keen awareness of my imminent departure.

" Ah bring something for yuh doh," he stated, presenting me with a modestly wrapped package.

" Wha's dis?" I queried, gently exploring the parcel's contents through tactile examination.

" Well, open it nuh, yuh go see for yuhself," he urged, observing my reaction with interest.

" Is ah going away present boy," he chuckled modestly. " Yuh could call it ah gif ah wamt if yuh want."

With each word, his gaze shifted enthusiastically, and his smile clung to the contours of his elongated face.

" Ah wasn't trying to name it unless yuh wah meh to," I quipped.

" Is up to you if yuh want to be de Godfader," he replied in jest.

" Before ah name it anyting doh, ah ha to see wah it is," I responded.

" I en't stopin yuh; open the ting nuh, yuh go see for yuhself," he replied with growing impatience.

" Ah gif of wamt eh?" I muttered as I unwrapped the package.

Within lay a short, gently worn fur garment reminiscent of a small brown bear's hide.

" Wha de hell is dis?" I queried.

" Is ah winter coat boy," he responded, his face brimming with anticipation.

" Yuh right," I acknowledged. " We should give it ah name."

" Whappen, yuh never see ah winter coat before?" he quizzically remarked.

Indeed, I had never encountered such an item close.

"Try it on nuh," he insisted.

I donned the coat and appraised my reflection in the mirror.

" Yuh like it?" he inquired.

"Yeah, it nice," I affirmed.

" Way yuh get dis from?" I inquired.

" Whappen, yuh tink ah tief it or wah?" he retorted wryly.

" Nah man," I reassured him. " Ah jus axin."

" Ah used to wear it when ah was livin in Bermuda," he divulged.

" It does snow in Bermuda?" I asked incredulously.
" Nah man, but boy, in the evenin over day does get real cole," he explained.
" Ah doh need it no more so ah bring it for yuh," he concluded.
" Is ah good ting yuh bring dis; because ah en have nottin to keep meh warm when ah reach up dey, not even ah woman," I jested, eliciting laughter from us both.
" Yuh know yuh's meh boy, right?" he affirmed, his smile underscoring the sincerity of his sentiment.
" If yuh want it, is yours," he offered.
"Tanks," I responded. "It nice."
"So yuh want it or not?" He inquired.
"Yeah," I replied. Ah tink ah go take it."
Vincent and I became friends not long after he had returned from Bermuda. New to the insurance industry, I volunteered to show him the ropes until he was comfortable enough to venture out on his own. Frequently riding shotgun with me, he learned the job quickly and since he did not own a vehicle, he became my constant companion. On a few occasions, I had assisted him with matters of a personal nature and thought nothing of it. However, he saw this as an opportunity to repay a debt that I didn't think he owed. It was clear that giving this garment to me meant a lot to him, so I gracefully accepted it.
" Boy, ah hear it does get real cole in Canada yuh no, dis go keep you from freezing to det wen yuh reach up day."
"Tanks again," I said. Ah sure it go comeen handy when ah reach way ah goin."
"Yuh go be glad yuh have it," He assured me.

"Upday does get reeel cole boy, reeel cole."

To emphasize the severity of the cold, he repeated the phrase "reeel cole."

" Dah cole kill better man dan you yuh no," he jested.

" Ah wasn't planning to dead," I responded in jest.

" I wasn planning to dead, nider," he concurred.

Vincent, a long-time resident of Bermuda, attested those temperatures plummeted precipitously after nightfall.

"Between me an you, if I didn't have dis coat boy, dah cole wodda kill meh long time," he confessed in a moment of vulnerability.

Recognizing Vincent's penchant for embellishment, I took his statement with a grain of salt.

" Well, ah glad yuh didden dead, cause yuh wooden ketch meh dead in a dead man coat,'" I quipped, eliciting mutual laughter.

"It fitting rite," I remarked as I admired the coat.

" Ah feel like ah ready for de cole," I declared. " Ah cah wate to put it on when ah reach up day."

" It look good on yuh," he remarked. " Yuh really like it?"

" Yeah! Ah go take it," I affirmed.

" Den leh we call dat George den," he declared.

" If yuh insist on naming it, George is as good a name as any," I conceded.

"OK. Call dat George," he replied, signifying the conclusion of the matter.

" Yuh want a beer?" I asked, changing the conversation.

It was a query to which I already knew the answer. Having worked alongside Vincent for over two years, I was aware of his fondness for alcohol.

" Yuh no I cah say no to something cole," he confirmed.

" Wah yuh want, ah Carib or ah Stag?" I inquired, knowing his preference mattered little.

Hedging his bet he replied, " Ah go take ah Carib, buh if you eh ha dat, Ah go take ah Stag."

" An if ah ent ha Stag?" I pressed.

" Yuh ha Babash?" he queried, hopeful for a positive response.

" Nah! Ah jus joking," I replied.

As we cracked open our beers, our conversation meandered through topics ranging from Canada to Bermuda, punctuated by laughter and camaraderie. Although Vincent had never visited Canada, he spoke with authority about the country.

" How come you know so much bout Canada?" I probed.

" Ah have ah set ah family up dey boy," he revealed. " Dem does tell meh wah goin on."

" When was the last time yuh talk to yuh family in Canada?" I inquired pointedly.

He pondered for a moment before responding,

" Boy, dat was a few years ago yuh know. We doh really talk dah much."

" Is true," I empathized. " Ah understan wah yuh sayin. Even wen day rite here, it does be hard to keep up de the communication."

" Yuh no wah ah mean?" I replied, seeking confirmation while absolving him of any guilt.

As the night wore on and one beer followed another, alternating between Carib and Stag, Vincent continued to share anecdotes from his life, many of which I had heard several times before. He recounted his marriage, the inability to purchase property in Bermuda due to his non-citizen status, and the strain caused by their failed attempts at parenthood. His drinking escalated as the marriage deteriorated, leaving him with neither land, nor children, nor wife. Vincent had been out of the country for many years, and while he was away, most of his immediate family had immigrated. When he finally returned, there was no one there to welcome him home. In a sense, he had become an orphan. Although our relationship was of a professional nature, it was not long before I informally adopted him. We became close friends partly because of the circumstance in which he had found himself, but mostly because he was a good and decent man.

We talked into the late hours until we were both inebriated beyond coherence.

" It done late ahready," I remarked. ", if yuh want yuh could sleep on de couch."

" Dah go be cool," he replied. " I cah make it home in dis condition. On top ah dat, it en ha nobody waiting day for meh."

We both laughed, retiring for the night in a state of inebriation.

Nature's Wrath

As the conclusion of the festive Christmas season approached in 1988, reflections regarding my departure from the country began in earnest. While the decision to embark on this journey had undergone detailed deliberation, I found myself grappling with the conviction that relocating was indeed the most thoughtful course of action. Canada held promise, yet its opportunities demanded significant personal sacrifices, foremost among them the wrenching separation from my children. Despite this emotional toll, the allure of lucrative employment prospects and improved educational offerings lessened my concerns to some extent, although the impending separation continued to weigh heavily on my heart.

To divert my thoughts from the emotional upheaval of immigration, I turned my focus to the fundamental forces, particularly the weather, which had recurrently shaped my existence. The escalating heat and humidity on the island had become increasingly stifling with each passing year, necessitating relief beyond the customary seawater immersion. In hindsight, I am now inclined to attribute this extreme change in temperature to global warming, although this phenomenon had not yet entered our vocabulary nor saturated the consciousness of the society.

As the departure date loomed nearer, the prospect of experiencing the full spectrum of four distinct seasons, in contrast to the wet and dry seasons with which I was intimately familiar, grew ever more enticing. To occupy my time, I entertained thoughts of leisurely strolls in the fall among radiant vegetation, my scarf flapping rudderless in the wind. I envisioned myself adorned in wintry attire, enveloped by gently descending snowflakes, footprints marking the trajectory of my passage in the snow. Amid the relentless humidity, these musings gained intensity fostering eager anticipation for the embrace of cooler climes.

Adhering to airport protocols, I arrived well in advance of my scheduled departure time in January 1989, amid the onset of the dry season, which exacerbated the oppressive atmospheric conditions on the island. The delay of my flight, a common occurrence, compounded my sense of irritability, fatigue, and exhaustion. In the interim, my reflections drifted to recollections of weather-related calamities that had punctuated my life's narrative.

One such memory was the seismic upheaval of an earthquake in the 1960s, which shattered the tranquility of the early morning hours. The alarming rumble, akin to a runaway locomotive hurtling towards our house, provoked primal fear as it reverberated through the community. We were small children, huddled tightly together as the earth-shattering noise struck fear into our little hearts, but no one made a sound. Wide-eyed and paralyzed with the fear of not knowing, we huddled even tighter in the darkness. Pots and pans were falling with a clattering noise, compounding our fear. Failing to uproot the foundation of our house but not for lack of trying, the earthquake gave up, but it was not finished with the neighborhood. The violent rumbling continued in the distance, moving further and further away, until it was heard no more.

In the immediate aftermath of the earthquake, an eerie silence ensued and not a word was spoken among us. Even the usually punctual and rambunctious rooster had lost his courage to crow. Afraid to disturb the silence, he declined to announce the dawning of the new day. Though mercifully brief, earthquake's alarming impact left an indelible imprint, underscoring the instability of our existence amidst the turbulence of nature's wrath.

In the Caribbean environment, characterized by its bipolar weather patterns, both the wet and dry seasons harbor potential perils. Having weathered nearly three decades on the island, I remained acutely aware of the fickleness inherent in its climatic changes. The dry season, with its extreme heat reminiscent of Dante's Inferno, created an oppressive environment akin to an unrelenting fire. Conversely, floods of biblical proportions during the wet season evoked recollections of Noah's Ark with a deep sense of utter helplessness.

Reflecting on a flood encountered while travelling through the town of San Juan, I vividly recalled the sudden transformation of blue skies into a gloomy blanket, heralding the flood's onset. One moment the sky was cerulean blue before a thick dark cloud covered it like a canopy. In an instant, day became night as thunder rolled across the sky like massive boulders, followed by daggers of lightning that ripped the dark cloud open, releasing thick sheets of water. The old drainage system built during the colonial era and dire need of replacement, was incapable of accommodating the vast amount of water that had fallen in a relatively short time. Within minutes the streets became a raging river, overflowing with garbage and congested with traffic, triggering chaos. The water rose quickly, and drivers took to the roof of their vehicles to escape the deluge. Vehicles began to show signs of instability as if preparing to drift downstream. I was standing outside my car when a slightly built woman of East Indian descent was being carried away by the raging water.

"Oh God, Oh God, ah go drong." She screamed hysterically.

"Help somebody! Somebody help me!"

She was desperately trying to secure her footing, but the gushing water proved too strong for her slender build. I grabbed her by the arm and pulled her towards me as the putrid water raged around us. She was still clinging to me when as suddenly as it began, the rain stopped, and the water that had covered the streets slowly drained away. As if to survey the damage, the sun emerged from behind the clouds to shine its light on the tons of garbage that littered the narrow streets. Even after the water had subsided, several vehicles were unable to start. Months later, exacerbated by the high temperature and stifling humidity, the offensive odor of rotting garbage lingered in my car like a poltergeist. Unable to cope with the nauseating stench, I sold my white Mitsubishi Lancer with imitation tiger skin seat covers for less than its estimated value at the time.

On another occasion, an ill-fated attempt to navigate a waterlogged thoroughfare resulted in a misadventure, as my motorcycle succumbed to the sunken ground of a road still under construction.

Torrential rain had fallen earlier that day, which usually causes severe flooding in certain areas. To save time, I took a road that ran parallel to the highway but was still under construction. Despite its rough condition however, I would have been able to get to my appointment and back within the one-hour lunch I was allotted. As if subjected to a relentless bombing campaign, the road was pitted with potholes, which in turn were filled with muddy water, making it impossible to determine their depth. Yet, against my better judgment, I decided to risk the crossing. The journey started well until I encountered a pothole that could easily have been mistaken for a lake. With my feet raised high above the pedals, I ventured into the water. Almost halfway across the pothole, the bike began to sputter, and before I could turn around, the engine shut down completely. Unable to maintain my balance, the bike capsized in the water, trapping my leg beneath it. Instead of offering words of encouragement, a young man that was traveling on a bus along the highway shouted,

"Wine up yuh window."

Despite such difficulties, punctuated by mud and drenched expression of grief, that moment of lightness characteristic of West Indian humour, served to sustain me amid nature's rapidly changing maneuvers.

Destination Bound

Several hours after the scheduled departure, the aircraft finally arrived to take passengers to their destination. Hungry and exhausted, I ascended the stairs and was greeted by a stunning flight attendant with a captivating smile.

"Welcome aboard," she cordially expressed as she received my boarding pass and directed me to my seat.

With this swift exchange and a subtle smile, she turned to the next passenger, maintaining a poised and professional demeanor throughout. Although her disposition was pleasant, and business-like, I was immediately smitten. Her deep dimples and almond-shaped eyes could have led me to her parlour like the cautious tale of the spider and the fly. Searching for my seat, I had a feeling that I had seen her before, maybe in a toothpaste commercial, but I could not be certain. I thought of the advertisements for Colgate, Aim, and Pepsodent, the brands that had dominated the local market for several years, but I still couldn't place her. It was only after I was securely seated that her smile softly faded, leaving me with no resolution. In the air-conditioned comfort of the aircraft, I focussed on the journey ahead. The anticipation of encountering winter, unfamiliar to my tropical upbringing, loomed as we embarked on our flight path to Canada.

With the aircraft soaring smoothly at cruising altitude, the announcement of lunch service brought relief to my hunger. The meal, surprisingly satisfying, accompanied by several glasses of wine, alleviated the fatigue of the journey thus far. Absorbed in the in-flight entertainment, I found myself momentarily lost in relaxation. By then my head was floating freely above my shoulders. Drifting in and out of an intoxicating food-induced coma, I casually dismissed the fact that I was careening through the air in an aluminium tube at 900 km an hour, 30,000 feet above sea level. With no milepost to indicate distance nor object to mark the passage of time, I had the strange sensation that we were suspended in space. I must have dozed off when the disturbing images to which I had previously referred began in earnest.

However, as the landscape below transitioned to a snow-covered expanse, the reality of the unfamiliar terrain began to set in. Despite initial reservations, the stark beauty of the snowy landscape captured my attention, though it drastically contrasted with the familiar tropical landscape of the island that I was leaving behind.

Notwithstanding the occasional turbulence we encountered along the way, the flight to Winnipeg was relatively smooth. Although it felt like forever, a mere four hours after leaving the island, we were cruising over the Province of Manitoba where the landscape exuded a strange beauty, and yet it seemed inhospitable and unfit for human habitation. Compared to the tropical paradise in which I had grown up, this was an alien planet. There was no sunshine, no leaves on the trees, no seawater, no sand, no mountains standing tall in the distance, nothing but snow and ice as far as the eyes can see.

Scattered widely across the snow-covered landscape were several tiny houses with ribbons of steam rising lethargically from their chimney tops. This reminded me of the houses often depicted on Christmas cards and fairy tales, scenes that I had always interpreted as visual representations of the illustrators' imagination. It surprised me to realize that these structures were the actual homes of human families. Although the decision to immigrate was based on empirical evidence, I had not considered the harsh reality of winter, with which I had no previous experience. This omission left me totally unprepared for what I was about to encounter.

Contemplating the radical change in scenery, I found myself drawn into a hypothetical reflection on cultural adaptation, pondering how narratives might differ had circumstances been altered. Fascinated by the snow, I thought of the many fairy tales that had delighted me as a child and wondered how the story would have unfolded had the Dwarfs stumbled upon a Black man instead of Snow White.

"Would they have been as accommodating to me as they were to her"? I wondered.

If not outright hostile, I imagined that they would be afraid. As my mind drifted and the scene unfolded, they huddled, speaking in hushed tones, debating the fate of the strange creature they had encountered. I was not of their kind, and neither did I look like anything they had ever seen before. Musing about this alternative scenario, a dwarf mustered the courage to approach. Short and stout with red bulging eyes, a long white beard, and a bulbous nose, he looked exactly as depicted in fairy tale illustrations. His was not a face that could be describe as remotely handsome nor even one that only a mother could love. It was as if a child had fashioned his features out of play doh and stuck the pieces in all the right places, before abandoning the project for another toy. His sizeable red nose suggested that he may have been out in the cold for an extended period, or he had consumed more than a few of his favourite beverage. Holding a stick much taller than himself, a weapon for defence, if necessary, he pointed towards a forested area far in the distance.

"Is Yooou frooom da dak fooores bee?" He shouted, displaying more teeth than his mouth could comfortably accommodate.

"No," I replied, modulating my voice so as not to alarm him.

"Nooooo!" He exclaimed, as if questioning the legitimacy of my response.

His voice echoed across the landscape, making him appear fearsome and more intimidating. His mention of the Black Forest made me wonder if he was associating the colour of my skin with the forest in question. To assure him that he was in no danger, I continued.

"I've never heard of the Dark Forest," I said.

Emboldened by my subdued response, he ventured closer.

"Showee yo handoo meee! He demanded.

"What?" I responded, unable to fully comprehend his command.

He extended his hand and repeated the words with increasing aggravation.

"Showee yo handoo meee! He shouted.

"You want me to show you my hand? I inquired.

Visibly angry, he repeated the command,

"Showee yo handoo meee!

Although uncertain of his intention, I complied and reluctantly extended my hand as he had demanded. With his bloodshot eyes fixed firmly upon me; he rubbed his stubby fingers hard against my skin. Then he looked at his fingers and confusion enveloped his face. Undeterred, he repeated the action with increased vigour, but the result was the same. The black from my skin did not rub off as he must have assumed. Panic stricken; he ran towards the group that were observing our interaction from a safe distance. Suddenly, a collective gasp erupted from within the group, causing the hair on my skin to stand up. Then a command was given, and before I realized what was happening, they were advancing towards me menacingly, armed with pitchforks and other crude weapons of war. If they attack like a pack of wolves, I thought to myself, despite their diminutive size they could inflict severe damage. I was about to run when the wheels of the aircraft connected with the tarmac, jolting me back to reality. The abrupt return to earth dispelled any lingering contemplation while clearly marking the beginning of a new chapter in a land, though unfamiliar was filled with promise.

Welcome to Winnipeg

Upon safely landing and disembarking the aircraft, I promptly retrieved my luggage from the overhead compartment and proceeded towards the baggage claim area. Awaiting the arrival of my belongings, I donned my "gif of warmt", to stave off the chill of the Canadian winter. As a member of a visible minority within a predominantly Caucasian society, I remained determined in pursuing my goals, undeterred by any potential obstacles whether real of imagined. Reflecting on stories of discrimination and pondering the potential challenges ahead, I reflected on the hazards of residing in a city with a history of racism against people of colour. Once again, I thought about the Dwarfs and how our interaction had unfolded. I wondered if living in this city would be any different from that imaginary encounter. It is one thing to be a tourist in a city, but when one must live among people with a history of discrimination, that becomes a horse of a different colour. As a man of African ancestry residing comfortably in the castle of my skin, I will have no choice but to decline, if the price of passing necessitates changing who I am.

Despite being the sole person of color amidst fellow travelers, I resisted entertaining fleeting doubts regarding the delay in retrieving my luggage, opting instead to focus on pragmatic concerns. Assuredly, my sponsor Phyllis, a white Irish woman married to a black man, awaited my arrival outside the airport terminal. Her assistance would ease my transition, underscoring the unconfirmed nature of any apprehensions regarding discrimination. Hence, I swiftly dismissed such notions, redirecting my attention to the practical implications of possibly losing my luggage.

Though only briefly clad in my winter attire, I noticed a slight perspiration, a testament to the coat's effectiveness against the elements. Vincent's endorsement echoed in my mind, reaffirming the garment's efficacy in combating the Canadian winter.

Although I was born and raised under the scorching heat of the tropical sun, I had a rudimentary understanding of what it feels like to be cold. As a child, I often played in water until my fingers became numb and wrinkled. Then I was left to stand against the wind naked, covered in goose bumps, teeth chattering and shaking uncontrollably. Now that I was wrapped in a warm coat and shielded from the wind, I was ready to fully embrace winter. Finally, my luggage arrived, and I was sweating profusely. I could no longer wait to feel the cool winter breeze caressing my face ever so gently. With luggage in hand, I made my way towards the exit but the door slid open before I was even close enough to touch it.

"This is some serious Star Trek shit," I muttered, "Beam me up, Scotty."

Then, like if by magic the second door opened and a wind, colder than anything I could ever have imagined, took my breath away and almost knocked me off my feet. Nothing that I had ever experienced in my entire life could have prepared me for the blast of Arctic air that accosted me so violently. Instinctively, I responded with a barrage of salty words that were muted by the cold, leaving me speechless and my mouth agape. The thoughts of snowflakes landing gently on my shoulders, that I had been harbouring for so long were immediately abandoned. Even the coat in which I was sweating profusely just moments before, provided no protection except to conceal my private parts.

Unprepared for the ferocity of winter and struggling to load my luggage into the vehicle, I grappled with the harsh reality of the climate. As the freezing wind intensified its assault, I found myself in a surreal struggle against the elements. The weight of my luggage was the anchor that saved me from being blown away. Exposed to the elements, I felt a burning sensation in my ear lobes and a numbness that took control of my extremities. Fearing that my ears and nose had fallen off, to confirm their continuing attachment to the rest of my anatomy, I touched them repeatedly. For the first time in my life, I saw my breath drifting away on a carpet of cold air, as if it too was desperate to escape the brutal assault. My entire body had become frozen, my legs had turned to stone, and I could no longer feel my toes. Like stalactites in the calcium-rich limestone of an underground cave, icicles of mucus hung disgustingly from my nostrils, attaching itself securely to my moustache, and beard. It was as if nature was interrogating me for a crime that I had not committed. My only crime was failing to dress appropriately for the weather, the intensity of which I could never have predicted. Although the penalty seemed worse than the crime, when nature is judge, jury, and executioner, there's no room for negotiation. The beautiful snow-covered landscapes in story books and Christmas cards gave no indication that a frigid assassin was lying in wait to ambush unsuspecting victims. This was not the winter that I had envisioned when I was anxiously waiting on the island for the plane to arrive. This winter had drained the heat from the sun and spread its frozen tentacles far across the land, ensnaring everything within its reach.

The lack of correspondence between the serene ambiance inside and the unfolding harshness outside the terminal building was evident. Reflecting on the ordeal, I concluded that the allure of Winnipeg's scenic charm belies its truly formidable and inhospitable nature. Contemplating the prospect of enduring such winter conditions as representative of a singular season, I found myself thinking about retreating to the inferno in which I was forged.

Eager to escape the bitter cold, my courageous struggle to stow luggage in the car's trunk left me yearning for warmth. Dressed in a thick golden fur coat sitting comfortably inside the vehicle, Phyllis exuded an aura of warmth and comfort.

"Are you crazy?" she exclaimed, her Irish brogue emphasizing her concern.

Startled by her animated reaction, I sought to understand the reason for her alarm.

"It's minus 45, and you are wearing a spring jacket!"

I had no idea that my Gift of Warmth was a spring jacket best suited for that time of year.

"Do you want to freeze to death"? She continued.

"It's too late now," I replied.

"It's not a laughing matter," she declared. "It's a matter of life or death."

"You're not kidding," I replied. "Five more minutes, and I would be returning to the island in a pine box."

"Is this what they mean by 'when hell freezes over'?" I quipped, attempting to diffuse the tension.

Yet, Phyllis's earnest response underscored the severity of the circumstances, dispelling any notion of light-heartedness.

"You need to get some winter clothes right now'," she emphatically declared, leaving no room for debate.

Acknowledging the necessity for immediate action, I agreed with her assessment, acknowledging the need for winter attire.

Despite the lack of feeling in my fingers, I managed to secure my seatbelt as we set off on a mission to Polo Park, Winnipeg's premier shopping destination. En route, Phyllis provided an overview on winter conditions, explaining the concept of wind chill and its aggravating effects.

"It is actually -35 degrees, but the wind chill makes it feel like 45 below." She said.

"What is wind chill?" I asked.

I was not familiar with the term, but I knew that it could not be good.

"Wind chill, she explained, causes the temperature to drop even lower.

"You mean that the cold intensifies when wind becomes a factor?" I inquired for the sake of clarification.

"That's exactly right," she responded.

As we navigated the bustling streets of the city, her insights into the realities of winter imparted a sobering realization of the challenges ahead. She sounded like a Meteorologist whose candid insight transcended enlightenment; it chilled me to the bone.

Although we had been stuck in traffic for more than half an hour, I was still frozen, fearing that my body would never know the warm embrace of sunshine ever again. Like King Richard in Shakespeare's Richard's III, I was desperate.

"A horse, a horse! My kingdom for a horse!" He cried.

Given the numbing effect of the cold, I would have given anything to feel the heat of the tropical sun against my melanated skin, even if it was only for moment.

"You never miss the water till the well runs dry," I said. "I bet no one has ever said that about winter."

"You'll be surprised," she responded as we pulled into the mall.

Arriving at the shopping mall, desperately in need of winter essentials; my focus was primarily based on functionality rather than style. With Phyllis's guidance, I put together a comprehensive ensemble comprising of a parka, gloves, earmuffs, winter socks, long johns, a toque, and a pair of heavy fur-lined boots to combat the elements. I had never heard of a toque, a parka nor long johns for that matter, but desperate circumstances demand desperate measures.

"These are winter essentials," she assured me.

"Great, I said. I'll take them,"

Sensing the finality in my response, she added with a subtle smile, "It's only a starter pack."

"You mean there's more?" I asked.

"There's always more, she intoned, but these will do for now."

Within hours of arriving in Winnipeg, I had transformed into a veritable embodiment of an Innuit hunter. Gazing upon my reflection in the dressing room mirror, adorned in layers of insulation, was a far cry from the loose clothing that I had worn throughout my life on the island.

Phyllis looked at me approvingly, as a mischievous smile spread across her elongated face.

"There is a reason why this province is often called Winterpeg you know," she said jokingly.

"It is cruel that I had to learn about that the hard way," I replied.

"On postcards, winter scenes are beautiful and that is very deceptive, is it the same with the occupants of this city?" I inquired.

"We have our issues, but you'll find out for yourself in time," she replied.

Phyllis's wry observation regarding Winnipeg's moniker as "Winterpeg" served as a gentle reminder of the city's reputation. Reflecting on the harsh lessons learned, I contemplated the parallels between the deceptive allure of winter scenes and the complexities of its inhabitants. As I embarked on my journey in this new environment, I braced myself for the challenges that lay ahead, guided by the wisdom gained from my inaugural encounter with Winterpeg's icy embrace.

Emerging from the underground parking facility, I found myself reflecting once more on the imaginary exchange with the Dwarfs, pondering the outcome of such an encounter. It was dark when we departed the shopping complex. Despite repeated efforts, the sun eventually conceded to the encroaching darkness. While the wind had abated, the snowfall had intensified. Our destination was Phyllis' residence in the Maples, a growing residential enclave situated on the shoulder of the city. At that moment, the evening rush hour reached its zenith, compounding the already treacherous driving conditions exacerbated by the accumulation of ice on the windshield wipers. With each sweep of the blades, frozen rain impacted Phyllis' vision, obscuring her navigation through the road ahead. The glaring headlights of oncoming vehicles and the slickened thoroughfares further exacerbated our perilous commute. Despite Phyllis' voiced grievances regarding the wipers and approaching headlights, she displayed a disconcerting nonchalance, borne of her familiarity with these circumstances over years of traversing similar routes. Only upon our safe arrival at her home did I finally exhale a sigh of relief.

The unmistakable scent of freshly laid carpet permeated the air of Phyllis' home as we entered. Amidst ceaseless chatter, she graciously offered me a cup of steaming hot chocolate, which I savored whilst accompanying her on a tour of her house. Before long, the strains of a lengthy journey, harsh wintry conditions, and impromptu shopping expedition began to take its toll, and I found myself unable to conceal my fatigue. Bidding goodnight, I retreated to a well-appointed room outfitted with a double bed, elaborate bedding, and plump pillows, providing a sanctuary of comfort. Exhausted, I succumbed swiftly to slumber, whereupon I was visited by dreams of playful escapades with my children in a sun-drenched park. With the arrival of dawn, I awoke in a winter wonderland, foggy and disoriented, with the Legend of the Cascadura on my mind.

The bed was now a warm cocoon, affording a moment for introspection amidst the sound of footsteps on the outside. Reflecting on the myriad blessings I had often taken for granted – family, friends, the sun, the sea, and the mountains – I found myself contrasted against the harsh reality of the wintry landscape, a stark departure from my tropical origins. Astonished by the determined spirit of the local denizens braving the elements, I couldn't fathom the rationale behind exposing children to such inhospitable conditions. While I pondered, nature beckoned, yet I hesitated, alarmed at the thought of youngsters frolicking in the snow, reminiscent of my own childhood escapades in the tropical rain. Whenever it rained, my mother would send us to school with plastic hats adorned with a variety of flowers; promotional items she received with every purchase of Five Roses. We despised those hats and as soon as we left the house, we yanked them off and stuck them in our book bags. With nothing to protect us from the weather, we sauntered to school in the pouring rain, drenched from head to toe, with not a care in the world. I wondered if these kids were having a similar experience like I did at their age. Although they were clearly having fun, laughing and throwing snowballs at each other, given the intensity of the cold, that seemed like a contradiction to me. Despite their apparent enjoyment, I remained skeptical, steadfast in my resolve never to subject my children to such inclement weather.

Thinking about the Cascadura's significance as a symbol of the immigration experience, I couldn't help but draw parallels between its perilous journey across dry land and the journey of humans leaving their ancestral homes for greener pastures. Like the Cascadura's trials in pursuit of a new home, humans are faced with cultural shock, marginalization, and discrimination as we seek a better life. Just as the Cascadura's black scales invite ridicule, so do people of a similar hue face scrutiny for their appearance, customs, and language. Yet, such challenges only fuel our determination to succeed. The succulent flesh of the Cascadura mirrors our internal beauty and the lands we leave behind. By infusing our talents and culture into new societies, we enrich them. Still, like the Cascadura yearning for its original home, we too long to return to our roots. This, I thought, encapsulates the essence of the poem—a metaphor for the immigration experience.

Deep in thought, I was again interrupted by nature's call which could no longer be postponed. Curious to see what damage the storm had inflicted; I reluctantly left the comfort of my bed to investigate. Peering through the window, I was dismayed to find that we were snowed in. Despite the darkness outside, the clock indicated morning. Concerned by the perpetual darkness, I observed people bundled up at a bus shelter across the street, realizing I hadn't anticipated such harsh conditions when leaving my sunny island home.

Determined to adapt, I immediately decided to acquire a vehicle.

"Winter could be as long as six months," Phyllis declared as she entered the living room.

"You want some coffee?"

"Coffee would be great," I replied.

A few minutes later she returned with two mugs that were piping hot.

"The thought of living with this weather for even one day frightens me enough," I said. "Six months would be the death of me."

"Winnipeg is one of the coldest cities in Canada." She said as a matter of fact.

"That's literally cold comfort to me." I replied.

"If you had mentioned that prior to my arrival, I may have chosen to stay at home in Paradise." I responded.

She laughed as if that was the funniest thing she had ever heard.

"You think here is cold," she continued, "wait until you get to Portage and Main."

"What about Portage and Main? I asked.

"Office towers in the downtown core have turned that intersection into a virtual wind tunnel." She responded.

"There's a pathway beneath the City Centre," she elaborated. "People can traverse the entire downtown area without ever surfacing."

"You should have led with that," I remarked.

While intrigued by this innovative solution to combat the weather, it finally dawned on me that I had chosen to live in the coldest city in Canada. Though hesitant to confront the weather, I realized I couldn't hibernate until winter's end. If others could adapt to this frigid environment, I owed it to myself to give it a shot before giving up. A few days later, bundled in winter gear, I boarded a bus bound for the city. As the bus navigated downtown, I mentally noted landmarks for my return trip. The bus wasn't crowded, and I, the only person of color on board, had a seat to myself, which didn't strike me as odd. Winnipeg's Black population is relatively small, so I didn't expect to see many people who looked like me. Then, someone requested a stop, and a woman I hadn't noticed before began to disembark. Upon reaching the exit, she turned around and, in a hysterical, high-pitched voice, screamed in my direction.

"Don't you come following me!" Her outburst drew the attention of all passengers.

I glanced behind to see who she was addressing, but no one was there. Her accusation was directed at me. This was my first day out in public and I felt like a criminal, subjected to an unfounded accusation that was deeply discomforting.

"She must have mistaken me for someone else," I reassured myself.

"Who does she think I am?" "Should I prepare for similar encounters in the future?" I wondered. "Perhaps I misjudged the city when I first visited in the summer," I reflected.

"Maybe the city is not as racially progressive as I assumed."

As these thoughts raced through my mind, an elderly white woman came to my defense, seemingly aware of my discomfort.

"Ignore her, dear," she advised. "She's not in her right mind."

While I couldn't speak for others, those comforting words from a stranger reassured me that at least one passenger didn't see me as a criminal. After the woman got off the bus and stood on the sidewalk, I realized she had what appeared to be Down's Syndrome. However, that is no excuse; she must have learned that racist behavior from somewhere. Following that incident, I wondered how often I should expect racially motivated attacks. Thankfully, it was the only time I was conscious of being racially profiled in Canada. The many acts of kindness I received from strangers since arriving in the country far outweighed that single incident that occurred years ago.

A week later, I was back in the city for an appointment, but was having difficulty finding my destination. In the Caribbean, directions are typically given in terms of Up, Down, Left, Right, or Straight. However, in Winnipeg, directions rely on North, South, East, or West. Confused about the cardinal points in relation to my current position, I approached an elderly gentleman for help, only to discover he was as clueless as I was.

"Come with me," he offered, briskly leading me to a nearby service station. "We'll sort it out together."

"No, it's fine," I protested. "I'll ask someone else."

"It'll just take a moment," he insisted. "Come on, let's go."

Reluctantly, I followed him into the gas station, where he asked the attendant for a city map. Together, we located my destination.

"Thank you for your help," I said, feeling grateful but also guilty for inconveniencing him.

"You're welcome," he replied. "It was no trouble, no trouble at all."

After cordially wishing me a pleasant day, he proceeded with his affairs, leaving me to contemplate the depth of his generosity. He easily could have claimed ignorance and continued his way without offense. Yet, as a denizen of the city, he likely recognized my newcomer status and deemed it his civic duty to help. Despite the inclement weather, his genuine willingness to aid was but one example of many acts of kindness that hastened my integration into the community. During my two-year tenure in Winnipeg, I encountered numerous individuals whose inherent decency and compassion bestowed upon the chilly metropolis a warmth that belied its climate. While insufficient to raise the mercury, their kindness accelerated my adaptation to Winnipeg far beyond my expectations. Such instances, alongside others of similar ilk, lend credence to the province's motto, "Friendly Manitoba."

A few weeks post my arrival in Winnipeg, I secured an apartment nestled in a picturesque neighborhood adjacent to the Assiniboine River, close to Osborne Village. Characterized by a blend of low and mid-rise residential complexes and majestic tree-lined streets, the area exuded a distinct charm. My apartment, conveniently situated within walking distance of my workplace, afforded glimpses into the lively nocturnal scene of the village. Even amidst the winter chill, cafes and restaurants teemed with activity, attracting patrons from afar to bask in the welcoming atmosphere.

Carlos and Murphy, a renowned Mexican-themed eatery in the village, swiftly became a favored haunt. Its inviting atmosphere and extensive menu, showcasing nachos, wings, and burgers among other delights, offered solace. However, despite the lively scene, a sense of absence lingered—a longing for a taste of home. While the atmosphere remained jubilant, the absence of Soca, calypso, and other cherished musical genres left a void, that failed to resonate with my cultural roots. Rock, pop, and country melodies dominated the festive soundscape, accentuating the realization that something essential was amiss, not merely within the village but within myself. The absence of these familiar rhythms served as a poignant reminder of my heritage and contributed significantly to my discomfort.

In February 1989, as Trinidad celebrated Carnival, I couldn't shake the sense of longing. The months of preparation that culminated in two days of music and masquerade on the streets of Port of Spain had no impact whatsoever on the city.

Neither did the pre-carnival activities that leads up to this annual extravaganza featuring elaborate costumes, amazing colour, and intoxicating music. There was no coverage by the local media of the carnival celebration that was taking place on the island. While the streets of Port of Spain were on fire, the City of Winnipeg was completely immersed in ice and snow. Plodding through the snow on my way to work with images of scantily clad women jumping up in the streets of Port of Spain was the closest I could get to the musical extravaganzas that had taken over Port of Spain. I recall playing mas one year as a member of the band, Harem. In this portrayal, I assumed the character of an Arabian Sheik, encircled by a group of elegantly attired women adorned in flowing silk garments, their presence adding a captivating allure to the spectacle. Positioned atop a flatbed truck, with makeshift Bedouin tent, we indulged in an extravagant display, replete with an abundance of refreshments, culinary delights, and, most notably, enchanting melodies. It was not merely the libations that stirred the senses, but the rhythmic pulse of Sparrow's "Drunk and Disorderly" and Shadow's "Baseman from Hell" that ignited the thoroughfares of Port of Spain with fervor and excitement. As if in a trance, I heard the music and saw the masqueraders in all their glitter and glory, parading through the streets of Port of Spain. While in this state of euphoria, oblivious of my surroundings, I stepped on a patch of ice, and landed hard on my behind, the contents of my briefcase scattered in every direction. Cursing profusely beneath my breath as I returned to reality, I leaped up, gathered my documents, and without breaking stride, continued as if nothing had happened. I had sustained no physical injuries, but my heart and spirit felt like they were irreparably broken, and I feared they could never be put together again.

"What the hell am I doing in this God-forsaken place on Carnival Monday?" I asked, frustration taking hold of me.

After residing in the city for over two months, I found myself still struggling to adapt. Seated alone at my desk, a profound sense of melancholy enveloped me, prompting me to question once more the wisdom of my decision to leave a sun kissed island for a land of ice and snow. While my colleagues casually accepted what to them was just another manic Monday, for me, it felt as though I had entered a realm of desolation. In the ensuing days, I grappled with waves of nostalgia, a condition I knew could only dissipate with the passage of time.

As the long, somber winter gradually receded, subtle signs of spring emerged, offering a tangible testament to the city's metamorphosis. Almost overnight, delicate buds unfurled on the trees adorning my street, while blades of grass defiantly pierced through the recently frozen ground, heralding the return of vitality. Beneath the canopy of branches lining the thoroughfare, thousands of verdant caterpillars descended, providing a welcome feast for the many small birds that ravenously devoured them. With each passing day, the grip of winter's gloom loosened, and I bore witness to the rejuvenation of the earth, an awe-inspiring spectacle unfolding before my eyes in real time. This palpable transformation infused me with renewed vigor, signaling the imminent arrival of summer as the final vestiges of snow melted away.

Before long, restaurant terraces usually filled with customers, overflowed with patrons once more. Street performers captivated audiences with their artistry, and sunbathers reveled in the warmth of the season's embrace within the verdant parks. The city had sprung to life, revealing to me once more, the profound reverence Winnipeggers hold for the sun. The innate splendor of my surroundings became even more pronounced, rekindling fond memories of the Winnipeg that attracted me on my exploratory visit in the previous summer. Despite the lingering chill that still sends shivers down my spine, my year spent in the vicinity of Osborne Village nurtured within me a deep-seated affection for Winnipeg.

Determined to establish a presence within the city, I immersed myself in the West Indian community of Winnipeg. Word of my recent arrival spread swiftly, resulting in frequent invitations to private dinners and social gatherings. Week after week, I found myself surrounded by an array of West Indian delicacies such as macaroni pie, stewed chicken, callaloo, paleau, souse, roti, and more, reminiscent of the comforts of home. It was apparent that my arrival as one of the few recent West Indian immigrants had sparked considerable enthusiasm among the Caribbean populace in the area.

These invitations not only facilitated my integration into a vibrant social network but also provided opportunities to solidify relationships. To further broaden my connections, I became involved with the Winnipeg Steel Orchestra and the Winnipeg Folk Choir. Established by longstanding Caribbean immigrants who had settled in the city decades earlier, these organizations boasted a diverse following comprising individual from various racial and ethnic backgrounds. The willingness of members to brave the harsh winter conditions to attend practices underscored their unwavering dedication to preserving Caribbean culture and fostering community spirit.

Among the notable figures within this community were Joan and Gene, a dynamic couple considered pillars of the West Indian community. Their fervent passion for Caribbean folk music and culture had a profound impact on those around them. Joan had been a member of the renowned Mousica Folk Choir in Trinidad before immigrating to Canada. Her dedication to preserving and promoting Caribbean folk music led her to establish the Winnipeg Folk Choir, where she served as musical director for several years.

Joan, with her striking presence, exuded sophistication, and charm. Her complexion, reminiscent of sun-ripened peaches, complemented her pleasant demeanor, striking appearance, and melodic voice, earning her admiration from all quarters. Not only was she a local luminary to be proud of, but she also contributed to the community as a schoolteacher and chair of the Winnipeg chapter of The Congress of Black Women. Joan's unwavering commitment to keeping the flame of Caribbean culture alive in the city earned her widespread respect and admiration.

A strikingly handsome individual from Trinidad, Gene, Joan's husband, held the esteemed position of primary school principal while also serving as Chair/Member on various boards. Active within the Folk Choir and providing vital support to the Winnipeg Steel Orchestra, Gene was a multifaceted community figure.

Similarly, Ruthven, another native son, embodied a gentle demeanor and possessed a deep-seated passion for music. Like Gene and Joan, he too dedicated himself to the teaching profession and played an integral role in the choir. Serving as captain of the steel orchestra, Ruthven brought musical accompaniment to life on the Second Pan during performances. His love of the art form and quiet disposition attracted people of all ages and all walks of life to join the steel orchestra.

Together, we endeavored to share the vibrant spirit of Caribbean culture at community events and folk festivals throughout the province, introducing its warmth and melodies to new audiences. Our repertoire included a rich medley of West Indian folk songs such as "Apre Carnival La," "Boykin," "Island in the Sun," "Jamaica Farewell," "La Rein Reve," "Liza," "Mangoes," and "Day O," among others.

Dressed impeccably in black pants and white frilled shirts with wide flowing sleeves, the men exuded sophistication, while the women adorned themselves with white headscarves and ankle length vibrant floral dresses, creating a visual spectacle.

Our performances were met with excitement, admiration, and genuine appreciation from audiences, who were often amazed by our presentation.

Though their names may not grace the annals of Winnipeg's history, the undeniable contribution of Gene, Joan, Ruthven, and their companions to the city's cultural tapestry and quality of life remains a testament to their enduring legacy.

Through their leadership, we shared our music and traditions with audiences across the province, bridging cultural divides and spreading joy wherever we went. Despite the bitter cold that enveloped the city, their warmth and hospitality made Winnipeg soon feel like home. And as I reflect on my time there, I realize that it was their kindness that helped me embrace the city, thawing the icy exterior to reveal its true warmth.

As if to compensate for the long, harsh winter, the city burst into vibrant life with the arrival of summer, marked by a plethora of public events. Among the most eagerly anticipated was Folklorama, a jubilant celebration of arts and cultures from around the globe. Over two consecutive weeks in August, diverse cultural organizations showcased their talents at pavilions scattered across the city. With a "Passport" granting access to all performances, attendees could embark on a global journey without ever going beyond the city limits. Throughout the festivities, the air resonated with melodies from distant lands, while the tantalizing aromas of international cuisine mingled enticingly. Folklorama served as a gateway to learning about cultures that might otherwise remain undiscovered, sparing individuals the expense and effort of extensive travel.

Among the myriad summer events, none garnered as much anticipation as Caripeg, a vibrant homage to Trinidadian carnival culture. People looked forward to this annual event, the human equivalent of spring that brings the city back to life after a long, cold winter. Caripeg connected people with a cultural experience, confirming their continued existence and making them feel alive again. Evolving into a grand spectacle over the years, Caripeg symbolized the city's reawakening after the bleak winter months. It provided attendees with an instinctual connection to their cultural roots, igniting a sense of vitality and renewal. Drawn from Trinidad, the US, and beyond, revelers flocked to partake in this annual extravaganza. Echoing the traditions of Trinidad carnival, Caripeg featured competition for the king and queen of the band, lively calypso tents, and the crowning of a Calypso Monarch. Throughout the day, bands paraded through the streets, beckoning participants of all ages like a modern-day Pied Piper. The pulsating music and infectious jubilation made resisting participation impossible. Later, as exhaustion set in, the festivities culminated in a final gathering at a local park, where music and dancing persisted unabated. Once the revelry had subsided, sanitation crews diligently set about clearing the remnants of celebration, unaware of the weighty burdens left upon the city streets during that day of intense life affirming revelry.

The Stage Beckons

Conversations in Winnipeg, often start with a nod to the weather, a shared acknowledgment of the frigid reality at Portage and Main, the city's coldest and most inhospitable intersection. When winter arrives, people would hunker down and pray for it to be over much sooner rather than later. Winter's grip leaves no one untouched, yet unlike creatures that can slumber through the cold, regardless of temperature, human beings must soldier on. This is particularly true of Caribbean immigrants accustomed to sun-kissed days and there were several consecutive days when the sun did not shine. To combat the stultifying effects of boredom and isolation, cultural groups emerged, their vibrant performances have been thawing frozen spirits for years and warming the hearts of many throughout the winter season. But even these stalwarts tire over time, for without the occasional infusion of new blood, a sluggishness ensues. Therefore, when a new person arrives in that province, it's like a ray of sunshine, a light that radiates even warmer, if that virtual stranger has experience in the theater arts.

I first met Mack in a downtown bar frequented by West Indian expatriates. As we swapped tales of blizzards and the infamous intersection of Portage and Main, our banter evolved into shared stories of adaptation. Although it was nothing to laugh about at the time, I told Mack of my experience with the weather when I first arrived. Not to be outdone, he shared a similar experience which created an instant bond between us as we doubled over laughing uncontrollably. During our conversation, I learned that Mack was the driving force behind a West Indian theatre group in the city that was founded in 1972. He spoke proudly about the many successful productions they had staged over the years but bemoaned a recent decline in enthusiasm. Despite months of rehearsals, he declared, they were struggling to breathe life into their upcoming production. Frustration hung heavy in his words, until a spark of inspiration ignited.

"By de way," he interjected, " yuh ever ack on stage?"

"Yeah," I replied casually.

"Really?" His curiosity piqued. " Wah kind of plays yuh did?"

" I was in a few productions," I shrugged modestly.

As our chat veered into a more probing direction, it occurred to me that this was no ordinary conversation, but a job interview in disguise. And so, I regaled him with tales of performances in the company of luminaries like Derek Walcott and Raoul Pantin. Mack hung on every word, eager for insight into a world beyond Winnipeg's frosty embrace. As our conversation wove through brief memories of CARIFESTA and encounters with literary icons such as George Lamming and the widow of Dr. Walter Rodney, Mack's enthusiasm bubbled over. He couldn't get enough, seemingly savouring every detail and asking for more.

"Tell me de whole story." He demanded.

"Well, I was a member of the Trinidad Theatre Workshop, founded by Derek Walcott," I revealed.

Mack's reaction bordered on reverence.

"Tell meh more bout dat nuh," he urged, hungry for details.

"The Trinidad Theatre Workshop was the leading theatre company in the country," I said, and he responded as if he had stumbled upon a God send. Picking his jaw from off the floor, he continued the interrogation.

"Really!" He exclaimed.

"Carry on." He insisted.

"In addition to the Little Carib Theatre, we performed at several local venues as well as some islands in the Caribbean," I said.

He couldn't contain himself.

"Wah else all yuh do?" He inquired.

I mentioned that I had acted in "Beef No Chicken," a play by Derek Walcott, Raoul Pantin's "Hatuey," and Earl Lovelace's "The Dragon Can't Dance," among other. He listened with rapt intensity earnestly probing for additional details.

"Who yuh ack wit on stage "? He asked pointedly.

I mentioned that I had performed with Errol Jones and Charles Applewhite and Brother Resistance and Andre Tanker and Shango Bacou and Claude Reid and Stanley Marshall and Errol Roberts and Jemma Allong, all of whom were household names in the Trinidad theatre scene at the time.

He was clearly impressed.

"Way alyuh perform outside Trinidad? He inquired further.

I mentioned that I was a member of the Caribbean delegation that travelled to Barbados in 1981 for the Caribbean Festival of Creative Arts (CARIFESTA). He inquired about the background of this festival, and I told him what I knew of it.

I said that CARIFESTA was conceptualized in Guyana in 1970 with the goal of bringing Caribbean artists and cultural practitioners together to share and exchange artistic experiences and expressions. The intent was to foster stronger ties within the region by promoting Caribbean unity. In this endeavour, cultural groups from across the Caribbean, including Jamaica, Haiti, Guadeloupe, and Cuba among others were represented. He was entirely captivated and inquired about some of the personalities that we had encountered. I mentioned that in Barbados, we met the widow of Dr. Walter Rodney, the author of 'How Europe Underdeveloped Africa," the blueprint for revolutionaries throughout Africa and the African diaspora. We talked about the murder of Dr Rodney on June 13, 1980, when it was alleged that a bomb he was carrying had detonated in his car. However, most people believed that his death was a political assassination, and although there were several suspects, the case has never been solved.

I told him that we also had the privilege of visiting with George Lamming, the renowned Barbadian author and intellectual whose many books include "In the Castle of my Skin" and "The Pleasures of Exile." The former being a coming-of-age novel in a rapidly changing society while the latter is a collection of essays that examines Caribbean politics, race, and culture in an international context. He couldn't get enough and insisted that I continue.

I spoke of the members of the Trinidad group comprising of Andre Tanker, Brother Resistance, Charles Applewhite, Errol

Jones, Claud Reid, Stanley Marshall, and a handful of women whose names I do not recall. We were accommodated in a school, and two classrooms with bunk beds were set aside for the members of the cast. I regaled him with stories about the event, like the night the police raided the school in search of marijuana but left emptyhanded and humiliated.

I told him of another incident that occurred in Barbados during CARIFESTA. We were travelling on a bus enroute to the performance venue with the Mount Diablo Drummers from South Trinidad. The bus was full of performers, and the drummers were locked in a rhythm, summoning Yoruba deities with the beating of the Bo, the Bembe, and the Umele drums. The drumming was hypnotic and deeply spiritual, creating a vibration that may have summoned a supernatural presence in the confined space. In our group was a Caribbean woman of Caucasian persuasion, a fixture in the local theatre scene. We were sharing a seat when suddenly, a member of the Mount Diablo delegation who was sitting behind us, grabbed he around the neck and began to choke the life out of her. Immediately, six able-bodied men descended upon him but despite their best efforts, they could not release his grip. They were struggling unsuccessfully, until an elder in the group spat in his hand and slapped the aggressor three times on his forehead with his opened palm. In an instant the assailant went limp, he seemed to have lost his strength as his arms fell away from her neck. When he finally came to, he had no recollection of what had happened. After it was over, no one spoke a word of the incident, completing the remainder of the journey in awe and absolute silence.

We engaged in speculation regarding the motivating factors behind his decision to target the lone white woman amidst a cohort of black passengers aboard the bus. Our speculation led us to consider the possibility that the entity summoned and inhabiting the assailant may have been that of an enslaved African spirit. This supposition prompts the notion that his actions might have been driven by a desire for retribution, stemming from the injustices suffered by him and our forebears during the era of slavery. As for his precise motives, they remained beyond our grasp, residing solely within the realm of conjecture.

I told him about sharing a bunk bed with Charles, who slept on the top bunk, while I occupied the bottom. Charles had a habit of smoking in bed when everyone was asleep. What made the situation even more curious was the rumour that Charles buttered his bread on both sides, showing no preference for one side nor the other. One night the cigarette fell from his hand and landed on the floor between the wall and our bunk. I was fast asleep when he climbed down and attempted to reach over me to retrieve his cigarette. Sensing a presence, I opened my eyes and was alarmed to see Charles hanging over me.

"What the fuck you doing?" I exclaimed in the darkness.

My outburst jolted everyone from sleep, and someone switched on the light to see Charles' long lanky body straddled across mine. There were ten of us in the room, everyone looking confused and trying to make sense of his unorthodox position in my bed.

Clearly embarrassed, he responded sheepishly,

"Meh cigarette fall behind de bed an ah was trying to pick it up."

The room erupted in laughter as Charles retrieved his cigarette and proceeded to smoke what was left of it. The story amused Mack greatly, and he, too, burst into an uncontrollable fit of laughter.

But it wasn't just the glamour of the stage that captivated him. It was the anecdotes of camaraderie and mischief, mingled with embarrassment as we reminisced about shared escapades and close calls. In that dimly lit bar, amidst the pungent smell of alcohol, clinks and the hum of conversation, a bond was forged. Mack found in me not just a fellow weather-weary soul, but a potential savior for his struggling theater group.

After composing himself, he asked.

"Wah play alyuh do?

"The Dragon Can't Dance," I replied. He asked about the play, and I gave him a brief synopsis highlighting issues of poverty, class, politics, race and how all those factors fermented a failed rebellion. Mack found the story amusing. After regaining composure, he inquired, "Yuh ever direk ah play?"

" Direk a play?!" I exclaimed, caught completely off guard by the question.

"Yes, direk a play," he reiterated.

His urgency surprised me; I thought we were just chatting, although it often felt like I was being interviewed.

" Ah donno bout dat," I replied honestly. " Ah was on stage plenty times, but ah never direk a play."

" Da's no problem," he assured me. " You's jus de man we lookin for."

Mack emphasized the urgency, lamenting their lack of readiness just weeks before the festival.

" Is jus a few weeks from now yuh know and nobody know dey blasted lines," he declared, clearly exasperated.

"It dam frustrating yuh know. To tell yuh de trute, ah was seriously tinkin bout calling it quits."

Despite his clear frustration, the idea of quitting seemed hollow. From our conversation, it was obvious that Mack was willing to do whatever it took to salvage the production.

" Dis is a big ting," he stressed, as if envisioning the unfolding events.

" We cah go on stage if we doh know we lines. We go look like ah bunch of fools and I cah deal wit dat. I raddar scrap de play than for we to go on stage an make a fool ah weself."He declared.

" You's de only man dat could help we now," he said with conviction. " You's we only hope."

Though I'd never directed before, Mack seemed convinced that my theater experience was sufficient for the task. Sensing the urgency and being presented with the opportunity to showcase West Indian culture in Winnipeg, I agreed to help. And so, I found myself directing "Calabash Alley" in 1989, finding a new stage on which to shine. The play was written by Freddie Kissoon, a renowned Trinidadian playwright, drama teacher, and actor.

Mack wasted no time; two days after our initial conversation, I was introduced to the cast as the new director. Coming from outside with theater experience sparked great interest and excitement in the group. The cast made more of my background and experience than was warranted, but given the urgency, I made no effort to correct them. Whatever Mack had said had captured their attention, and they welcomed me enthusiastically. No one questioned my credentials, neither did I raise the subject.

From the outset, it was evident the actors were disheartened. Their long-standing familiarity had dampened their enthusiasm for their roles, approaching the production without the necessary commitment. After being formally introduced, I expressed gratitude for their warm welcome and acknowledged their efforts in keeping West Indian theater alive in a cold and distant land. I acknowledged their efforts, mentioning that without their contribution to culture, the city would be a much colder and inhospitable place. They laughed and responded with applause.

" The play is a good one," I assured them. " I've seen it performed before, and I am looking forward to your help in bringing it to the Canadian stage."

Perhaps invigorated by the opportunity, they nodded and applauded enthusiastically. I assured them that despite the tight schedule, it was still possible to produce a play that would make our community proud. Their applause grew distinctly louder.

To compensate for my lack of directorial experience, I exuded confidence.

" Directing the play is not an issue, but it would be impossible to make it happen if you don't know your lines." They unanimously agreed.

Although I'd committed to Mack, I stated clearly that I'd only accept the role if they made a greater effort to learning their lines, which they promised. After formalities, we stayed around a bit longer getting to know each other and speaking about what was happening on the island. A few days later, we reconvened. They were ready, and I was about to make my directorial debut. We dedicated ourselves to putting on the best play possible. The excitement was palpable, and their acting experience made my job easier than I had initially anticipated.

The rehearsal space produced an electrifying atmosphere. Rehearsals were long and intense, often ending past 1 a.m. Yet, the actors returned each evening with increased enthusiasm. By the end of the first week, we'd made significant progress.

Because of their experience, the play came together quickly. During dress rehearsals, the set, sound effects, and costumes worked perfectly. Three weeks later, we were ready for the festival's opening night. It was then that the magnitude and calibre of the competition finally struck me. We were competing against theatre companies from across Manitoba and neighbouring provinces. Several of the troupes were headed by seasoned professionals who made their living in the theatre. Although Mack did mention that this festival was important, it had never fully registered. My major concern was to make the production happen. If I had understood the magnitude of the occasion and calibre of the competition we were up against from the beginning, I never would have agreed to direct the play. However, after working with the group for several weeks and sharing in their excitement, I had become emboldened. As Director, the actors had demonstrated their belief in my abilities and was looking to me for leadership. What's more, I was already in over my head, and my only option was to press ahead.

Being one of the opening acts, the pressure was immense, but we were ready to break a leg, as is often said in the business. For an entire week, we performed to sold-out audiences, receiving overwhelmingly positive reviews. Competing against seasoned professionals from across Manitoba and neighboring provinces, we held our own. There were over twenty professional troupes from diverse ethnic and cultural backgrounds competing at various locations throughout the city. Despite the slow start and the limited time that was available for rehearsals, in the end we were satisfied that we had done our job. When the curtain finally fell, there was consensus that the festival was a resounding success.

The awards ceremony was a gala event with speeches by distinguished local personalities. Being new to the city, I was not familiar with any of them but judging from the response they received from the audience, they must have been people of some significance. The standing ovations that we received during each performance suggested that we had put on an excellent play but had no idea if it had resonated with the judges. When the awards were given out, we were honored with several accolades, including Best Play and Best Director. On hearing the announcements, congratulations echoed throughout the ballroom and several high-profile people in the industry made it their duty to interduce themselves to us. We mingled with the crowd, and, for a moment, we were an integral part of the Winnipeg theatre establishment. Amidst the celebrations, we felt a sense of accomplishment and pride. Though I never pursued theater in Canada again, the memories of that remarkable production endure. What we achieved within that tight timeframe was unparalleled and remains one of the major highlights of my life's achievements. Any attempt to replicate it would have been extremely difficult, if not impossible to surpass.

Winter Weather

While waiting for my family's documents to be processed, I worked as an Insurance Broker at Mutual of Omaha. Engaging in community fairs and events became my avenue to generate business leads. One such event led me on a journey to Thunder Bay on the shore of Lake Superior, a route spanning 700 km or an eight-hour drive from Winnipeg. By then I had been living in the city for several months and was looking forward to seeing Lake Superior, allegedly the largest freshwater lake in the world and the great Canadian Prairies, both of which I had read about in high school Geography. Because I had been working feverishly, I felt that the drive to Thunder Bay would free my spirit, giving me that long overdue break that I desperately needed. It was relatively early in the fall when I embarked on this journey and the thought of seeing the Canadian Prairie where wheat, maize, and soybeans grow in abundance was thrilling. To arrive at my destination however, I had to travel along the Trans-Canada Highway, allegedly the world's longest national highway spanning 7,821 km. Cell phones and GPSs were not available at the time, so with a map of the province and a spirit of adventure, I set out on my journey of discovery. To say that I was excited would be an understatement, elation is a more fitting term to describe my emotional state at the time.

Traversing the Trans-Canada Highway, I found myself amidst the breathtaking expanse of the Canadian Prairies with its vast and fertile fields. For miles along the extensive highway, autumn leaves in varying shades of red and orange, and yellow, waved in the wind. In rolling fields extending as far as the eyes can see, cows, horses, and llamas grazed lazily, pausing only briefly to survey their surroundings. With vibrant autumn hues adorning the highway and grain silos punctuating the prairie landscape like giant penises, it was as if I was traveling through a living canvas, each scene evoking a sense of wonder akin to a masterpiece by Vincent Van Gogh.

It was late afternoon when I finally arrived at my prospect's trailer on an Indian reservation. New to Canada, I was not fully aware of the deplorable conditions under which Aboriginal people lived. After briefly assessing the situation, I immediately knew that my prospect was not in a financial position to avail himself of my services. However, to convince myself that I had followed through on the purpose of my visit, I completed the interview. When the sale that I had driven for almost eight hours to secure failed to materialize, I was neither surprised nor disappointed. In addition to being exhilarating, the drive to Thunder Bay was itself a reward. Being away from the city liberated my spirit and gave me a much-needed mental break from the hustle and bustle of city life.

Upon concluding the interview in the early evening, darkness had already descended, prompting me to deviate from the original plan to return to Winnipeg. Instead, I secured lodging at a motel with the intention of further exploring Thunder Bay the following day. However, my plans were swiftly altered by the morning's weather forecast, which predicted a significant shift in conditions. Consequently, I made the decision to forgo exploration and commence my journey back to Winnipeg. The Prairie air was invigorating as I embarked on the highway, serenading the journey with the melodious strains of "What a Wonderful World" and reflecting on the joys of existence.

While traversing the Trans-Canada Highway, I was captivated by the spectacle of snowflakes, each as expansive as saucers, delicately landing upon my windshield. Their intricate formations and innate beauty elicited a sense of delight. However, my amusement soon gave way to anxiety as the intensity of the snowfall escalated rapidly. With each passing kilometer, the weather conditions deteriorated markedly. Despite my efforts to mitigate the obstruction posed by the snowflakes with the windshield washer fluid, the situation worsened as the substance froze, impeding visibility and rendering unsafe, the road ahead.

Just as I thought conditions could not deteriorate further, the precipitation transitioned into freezing rain, transforming the extensive Trans-Canada Highway into a treacherous ice rink and triggering chaos.

The perilous road conditions made it difficult to control the vehicle with the authority necessary to continue the journey safely. On both sides of the highway, vehicles of every make and model, including large trucks and tractor trailers had skidded off the road and ended up in the ditch. Soon, traffic began to pile up, making the situation increasingly worse. Rather than risk accidents, several drivers parked their vehicles on the shoulders of the highway to wait out the storm. With every passing minute, the storm increased in intensity, forcing the closure of the highway by the Royal Canadian Mounted Police (RCMP) and discarding any hope I had of advancing further. Not contented with parking on the shoulder as many had already done, I exited into a small community just off the highway where I found a motel. Given the amount of snow that was falling, I was certain that I would be stuck there for several days. However, by morning it was no longer snowing, the highway had re-opened, and I was able to continue my journey back to Winnipeg under a bright blue sky. This was the first time that I had ever experienced freezing rain and I swore to never to leave the city again neither in fall nor winter. But some things are easier said than done. Despite my vow to avoid winter travels, circumstances compelled me to brave the elements once more.

The documentation necessary for my wife and children remained in the hands of Canadian authorities, with an estimated processing time of eight to twelve months. These words resounded in my mind with the weight of a closing prison door. Prior to arriving in Canada, I had never been separated from my children for any prolonged. To ensure the proper attention to their paperwork, I maintained regular communication with the officer overseeing their case, receiving reassurances of diligent effort to facilitate our reunion. Meanwhile, 5,458 kilometers spanning land, sea, and sky separated me from my family, leaving me powerless to hasten the process but to endure the passage of time.

We were in the grip of winter when I was informed that the documents were ready and had to be picked up at an embassy outside of Canada. The nearest Canadian embassy to Winnipeg was in Minneapolis, USA. Although I vowed never to leave the city in winter, for fear of having the decision overturned for one reason or another, I refused to wait longer than necessary. Against my better judgment, I got into my car and headed to Minneapolis. I had been driving for a few hours when once again, a blinding snowstorm turned into freezing rain. To mitigate the risk of accidents and loss of lives, the Highway Patrol closed the highway. Again, I sought shelter in a motel in a small town to wait out the storm. From the comfort of my motel room, I watched the snow falling ever so gently. Yet, I couldn't help but think of how nature could be beautiful, brutal, and unforgiving all at once. Freezing rain and "black ice" can strike terror in the heart of anyone who encounters winter's wrath. This was particularly alarming since for all my life, I have lived in a tropical country and snow always looks so pretty on postcards. When viewed from the inside of a warm building, freshly fallen snow is stunningly beautiful. To ensure the roads and sidewalks were safe for drivers and pedestrians, salt must be applied to the surface. This causes the snow to melt and pools of water to accumulates everywhere. To cross over, one had to be a long jumper of Olympian status. A literal case of cold feet is when cold water gets into your boots. It's true that I was looking forward to experiencing the four seasons, but from what I had experienced so far, I've arrived at the conclusion that winter is one season I could live without. Reflecting on the beauty and brutality of nature, I realized the stark contrast between the picturesque snowfall and its treacherous consequences. Winter's harshness, a stark departure from my tropical upbringing, left me longing for the warmth of home.

With my family's documents secured, I made the journey back, resolving to delay their arrival until spring to spare them the bitter cold. It had taken almost one year for the documents to be processed and I couldn't wait to see my kids again, but winter was not yet over. For several weeks the temperature had been stuck at minus 35 degrees Celsius plus the windchill. Although I desperately wanted to be re-united with my family, I decided to delay their arrival until the spring. It would still be cold then, but not a bone chilling cold like the winter temperatures. I wanted to ensure that they would not have the same experience that I had when I first arrived. As I prepared for our reunion, memories of the time we were together intertwined with reflections on my childhood in Trinidad, reminding me of the island's warmth and vibrancy.

Reflections

Upon arriving in Winnipeg, I immersed myself in various activities to mask the ache in my heart. My children were far away from me, and my longing to reunite with them was palpable. They were the ebony fruits that had blossomed from the seeds I had planted a few years earlier, radiant offspring, rooted deep within my soul, my personal contribution to the propagation of humanity. Since their births, they had etched an enduring presence in my heart, resistant to the passage of time or the stretch of distance. Thoughts of them consumed me constantly, prompting questions of whether they felt the same yearning for me. I made a ritual of gazing at their photographs daily, to preserve the purpose behind my sacrifice, ensuring their faces remained vivid in my memory. Despite the anguish of separation, I found solace in knowing they were enveloped in love and care within the embrace of their mother, grandparents, and kin. Yet, for myself, there was no solace to be found when the weight of separation proved unbearable.

Stefan with his angelic countenance, plush lips, dark eyes, and tightly coiled locks, was a beautiful baby. His voracious appetite was evident as he eagerly consumed his milk, leaving bubbles at the corners of his mouth. Unfazed by his sister's slower pace, he would finish his feed swiftly, then doze off contentedly. He found pleasure in solitary play and would often fall asleep among his toys. Aware that the struggles of our people would one day be his own, I penned a poem expressing my profound love for him and my acknowledgment of the black man's journey.

Earth Angel

An angel came into the world one day in February,
His eyes were bright, his skin was soft, his hair was thick and fuzzy.
A blessing he just had to be, a blessing from above.
And as the years passed by, he simply filled my heart with love.
I tried to give him everything his little heart desired,
Nintendo games and basketballs, and books that I acquired.
The joy of learning he must know,
The wonders of the world,
That life is worth much more than just the silver and the gold.
The troubles we have had to face, the tears, the joy, the laughter.
For he would have to face them too from now and here on after.
So one day, when he has a child that fills his heart with joy,
He'll tell of all the things he learned when he was just a boy.

Gabrielle was a serene presence, with dimples adorning her cheeks and her smile causing them to deepen even further. Her ebony curls and dark eyes foretold a beauty still under construction. At her birth, her grandfather prophetically declared,

 "She go be ah craf," signifying her future allure as a beautiful and intelligent young woman.

Before his eventual passing at the ripe old age of ninety-eight, he adoringly witnessed her blossom into the vision he had foreseen many years ago.

Around the time of my departure, Stefan and Gabrielle were mere toddlers. Despite anticipating the ache of separation, I underestimated its magnitude. No amusement park ride could replicate the emotional roller coaster that I experienced ever since parting from them on the island. In my mind's eye, I saw them as vividly as if they were standing before me, their little faces lingering in my thoughts, each memory cherished with love and longing. The times we spent together were always special and when I recalled them, it was with love and deep affection. Like the moments shared watching "An American Tale," an animated movie featuring a young mouse and his family who were sailing to America to begin a new life. Essentially, the story was as immigration and adventure. Its theme song, "Somewhere Out There," became our nightly lullaby, reassuring them of my constant presence despite the distance.

On the day that I was leaving, we were on our way to their grandparents when a solemn atmosphere enveloped us. This was a journey that we had made several times over the past two years, and they were familiar with the routine. However, this would be the last time we'll be making this drive together and the thought of being away from them stirred me emotionally as I struggled to articulate the significance of the day to my young children, their understanding limited by age. Usually, they would be listening to nursery rhymes on route to their grandparents, but that day, the wheels on the bus did not go round and round. Instead, a deafening silence had permeated our mobile sanctuary, putting a damper on our usually joyful commute. Determined to extract the last precious moments from the little time that was left, I was in no hurry to arrive at our destination. The silence had become deafening and although they were toddlers, I felt the need to explain what this day meant for us as a family. They were not yet able to communicate fully and neither did they have any concept of time nor space. This made it difficult for them to articulate their feelings and for me to inform them of what was happening. However, my daughter's eyes have a penetrating quality that saw deep into my soul. Despite her limited vocabulary, she was able to convey emotions far beyond her linguistic capabilities at the time. Whenever I looked in the rare view mirror, her eyes would be fixed on me. It was as if she knew what I was feeling and wanted to comfort me. However, she lacked the vocabulary to express her emotions. Soon after getting into the car, Stefan had fallen asleep as he often did but Gabrielle was a trooper and a wonderful travelling companion. When she smiles, her dark eyes would usually sparkle but that day, there was no smile, no sparkle. Instead of her infectious laughter and angelic smile, she exuded a deep sadness. The depressions on both her cheeks where her dimples were prominently displayed were barely visible. She looked sad and it broke my heart.

After a long deafening silence, I summoned the courage to verbalize what I thought she instinctively knew.

"Daddy is leaving today," I faltered, feeling the weight of reality settle in.

My voice cracked and my heartbeat intensified as if trying to break out of its crimson chambers, to escape what was about to unfold. At that moment, I realized that I had never spoken those words before, and verbalizing had suddenly made it real.

"I'm going away today, Sugar Mugga," I repeated as if she had not heard me the first time.

Sugar Mugga was what I called her, a term of endearment with no real meaning except to say, "I love you." There was something sweet about it that always made her smile, except on this occasion.

"It will be a long time before I see you and your brother again," I continued as tears welled up in my eyes.

She looked at me consolingly as if she understood.

"Perhaps eight months or even a year," I continued.

Although she had no concept of time, she knew that things were about to change. On any other day, she would be gazing through the window, her little legs swinging back and forth like a metronome, in time with the beat of a nursery rhyme. Today I had her full attention.

"I'll call and ahh, ahhh I'll write every day," I stuttered.

Despite my best efforts to maintain my composure, the tears began to flow uncontrollably, obscuring my view of the road ahead. She looked at me consolingly and I knew that if she could, she would have said,

"Don't cry, Daddy."

But she lacked the vocabulary to convey such comfort. Yet her eyes spoke volumes. Through it all, she held strong, conveying emotions but never shedding a tear, even as I was being blinded by my own. Though her silence was profound, her presence was a source of strength, her unwavering gaze offering comfort amidst the turmoil while Stefan slept peacefully, unaware of the heartache unfolding around him.

Upon reaching their grandparents' home, I held them tightly, bidding farewell with a heavy heart. I kissed and hugged my children tightly as if I would never see them again.

"Take care of your brother," I said, discreetly wiping away tears with the back of my hand.

"Take care of each other." I said again.

Not wanting their grandparents to see me emotionally fall apart, I quickly bid them farewell, hugged them, and returned to the car dragging my heart behind me. On the way home, I thought of how they would react when I failed to show up at the end of the day. Usually, they would be waiting at the gate for me to shower them with hugs and kisses. I wondered how many times they would ask for me before I no longer existed in their memory. The heartbreak that I believed they would experience, rendered me inconsolable. The thought of not being able to hug my children for such a long time reduced me to tears once more. On my way home tears flowed unabated, aching for the moments we'd miss together. Their absence echoed in my soul; each mile home marked by the weight of our impending separation.

Time and distance can often conspire to focus the mind on events that were of little significance when they initially occurred. Yet, these were the moments that gave me comfort when I needed it most. From birth, Gabrielle and I had shared an unbreakable bond while Stefan found solace in his mother's embrace. On weekends, because he needed to be breastfed, he would often stay at home with mom while Gabrielle and I would go for long early morning strolls around the Queen's Park Savannah. This ensured that neither of us felt overwhelmed with the responsibility of caring for both children at the same time.

As a toddler, Gabrielle loved being outdoors but hated the confinement of her stroller. Determined to secure her freedom, she would wiggle until she eventually freed herself. Then she would stand on the arms of her stroller, laughing as if declaring victory. After several failed attempts to secure her again, surrendering to her spirit, I granted her the liberty she sought, a testament to the love that bound us together.

Once a sugarcane plantation, The Queen's Park Savannah has transformed into a multifaceted recreational hub, featuring a racetrack, cricket pitches, football fields, and various leisure facilities. It serves as the pulsating heart of Trinidad Carnival and offers an inviting space for physical activities or unwinding amidst its lush greenery. Carpeted in lush green grass and encircled by a 3.7 km tree-lined perimeter, The Queen's Park Savannah is reputed to be the world's largest roundabout. With the warm tropical breeze sweeping across the savannah, vendors selling corn, coconut water, snow cones, barbeque chicken, oysters, doubles, and other mouth-watering foods do a thriving business on its periphery, tempting passersby with irresistible aromas. It takes a tremendous amount of willpower to successfully resist the urge to indulge.

On its western fringe stand seven mansions, affectionately dubbed The Magnificent Seven or The Seven Sisters, dating back to 1902-1910. Some of these eccentric and flamboyant houses were built in late Victorian and other European styles, ranging from Baroque to Moorish, German Renaissance, and French Colonial, echoing a rich historical tapestry of our colonial past. Some also reflect a combination of multiple architectural designs. Though several are in a dilapidated state, they serve as poignant reminders of the island's heritage. Notable among them is Stollmeyer's Castle, rumoured to be modeled after Balmoral Castle in the UK and Queens Royal College (QRC), renowned for its academic excellence and sporting prowess.

In contrast to the elite institutions like St. Mary's College and College of the Immaculate Conception (CIC), which catered predominantly to the upper class, QRC welcomed students irrespective of race or economic status, nurturing intellectuals who transcended societal barriers. Notable alumni include Dr. Eric Williams, the first Prime Minister of Trinidad and Tobago, and C.L.R. James, a prominent Caribbean political philosopher and cricket writer. QRC also boasts of Sir. Vida Naipaul, Nobel Prize-winning author, Lloyd Best, economist, essayist, politician, scholar, and others, many of whom ascended from the bottom rungs of the socio/economic ladder and went on to international acclaim. The intellectual prowess of these young men enabled them to rise above the constructs of race and social class. Despite entrenched societal divisions, QRC fostered a legacy of inclusivity and academic achievement. These schools were a microcosm of the social, racial, and economic divide in the wider society. St. Mary's College and College of the Immaculate Conception (CIC) were the exclusive domain of the upper class, who were predominantly Whites, Chinese, and Syrians. A sprinkling of kids from other racial backgrounds were also admitted, often based on political connections or their family's socio/economic standing.

From as far back as 1923, QRC was a member of the Trinidad Amateur Football Association. Over the years, the college emerged as a dominant force in Inter-College football, more affectionately referred to as Inter-Col. This annual sporting event brought together thousands of fans from competing colleges across the country, each with their own unique characters. QRC's most notable character was a young man of considerable girth. Who, at random intervals throughout the game, would blow his trumpet as supporters repeatedly sang in unison,

"QRC, we want a goal."

QRC and St. Mary's Colleges were often in the Inter-Col finals. These schools were a microcosm of the wider society reflecting its social, racial, and economic divide.

On the northwest side of the savannah was The Hollows, a sunken area teeming with ponds of exotic tropical fish. The Botanical Gardens showcasing diverse flora lay adjacent to the

Hollows not far removed from the Emperor Valley Zoo. These serene sanctuaries provided solace for a young student, who, fearing the brutality of a tyrannical teacher, sought refuge in nature. Unknow to my parents, I spent many days in both the Hollows and the Botanical Gardens when I should have been at school. The fear of being brutalized by her created a tense atmosphere in the classroom, so I seized every opportunity to absent myself. I was so afraid of my teacher that my mind would go blank whenever she stood behind. Convinced that severe beatings stimulate learning, she'll apply the strap liberally and unmercifully. She ruled the classroom with a leather fist for at any moment, one of us could be severely beaten for offenses both real and imagined. Her inability to engage students usually resulted in severe corporal punishment. Recollections of juvenile escapades, including an encounter with a local ruffian, evoke a distressing nostalgia. More often than I care to recall, I ended up in the Hollows catching fish with a bottle and a piece of bread for bait. Whenever I strolled around the savannah with my daughter on our way to the Hollows and Botanical Gardens, this peaceful environment would trigger deep memories of my days as a budding juvenile delinquent.

Amidst these recollections, familial confrontations loom large, as I grapple with the consequences of absenteeism. During one of my escapades, I was fishing in the Hollows, unaware that a neighbour had seen me there when I should have been at school.

Interrogated by my stepfather, innocence crumbled under scrutiny, revealing the tumultuous interplay between youthful rebellion and familial authority. When my stepfather returned from work that evening, he asked,

"How was school today"?

"Good," I said, smiling innocently.

'It was good, eh," he replied.

There was a hint of sarcasm in his voice that told me there was more to the question than just his interest in my education.

'What you was doing rong de savanna dis mornin? He asked pointedly.

The blood drained from my face, and before he could say more, my eyes were filled with tears.

"Noting," I replied, my voice trembling, fearful of what was about to unfold.

"Noting eh," he repeated.

"So you was jus walking rong de savanna for notting, right?" He confirmed.

He was like a lion stalking its prey, coming in for the kill.

"So instead of going to school, you decide to go rung de savannah for notting, right?

"Yes, Daavid" I replied as tears streamed down my face and snot dripped from my nostrils.

"I sen yuh to school an you went rong the savannah for noting?

"No. I replied.

I was confused, unsure of how to respond appropriately.

"Come here," he demanded, his voice cutting through the air like a blade.

As my siblings gathered around, silently witnessing my impending punishment, I reluctantly approached him, each step a hesitant shuffle in a bid to postpone the inevitable.

"Han meh da belt," he commanded, his tone accepting no argument, gesturing towards the thick leather strap used to discipline us.

"Hurry up!" he barked; impatience evident in his voice.

Fear coursed through me as I trembled, anticipating the impending blows.

Daavid loomed over me like a colossus, his formidable presence accentuated by bulging muscles, bloodshot eyes, and veins pulsing beneath his skin. A man of physical strength, he had never needed to rely on a resume to secure work as a manual labourer; his imposing stature spoke to his ability. Among the many roles he had assumed over his lifetime, the task of meting out discipline seemed tailor-made for him.

A mere ten-year-old child facing the wrath of a giant, I felt even smaller and more fragile than I was while standing in his presence.

As I pondered how he could have known about my truancy, the reason faded into insignificance compared to the impending ordeal. Though his own education had been limited, he emphasized its importance to me, albeit in a manner that defied logic.

"This will hurt me more than it will hurt you," he declared solemnly, a statement I couldn't comprehend amid my fear.

Before I could unravel its cryptic meaning, the belt landed on my back with a resounding crack, sending waves of agony coursing through me. I writhed in pain, my cries echoing through the house as I crumpled to the ground.

"When I sen yuh to school," he said, "Dat is way I expect you to be."

He gripped my hand tightly, raining blows and lecturing me throughout the brutal episode. I may have been on the receiving end, but the lesson was intended for all my siblings.

"Oh, God. Oh God, Daddy David!" I screamed. "Ah wooden do it again!"

Amidst the onslaught of blows and lectures, I found myself calling out to God and questioning the justice of it all. But there was no reprieve, no divine intervention to halt the brutality, no justice as far as I was concerned. I was rolling on the floor, screaming, and begging for forgiveness, when my mother intervened to put an end to the savagery.

"David, ah tink dat enough, ah sure he wooden do dat again."

'You stay out ah dis woman," he shouted. "When yuh see I disciplinin dese children, you stay out ah it."

He shrugged her off, and although not a man of religious conviction, he added.

"Spare the rod and spoil the child."

However, my mother's steadfast voice cutting through the chaos, provided an opportunity to escape.

In the heat of the commotion, I ran out of the house. With nowhere to go, I literally slept in the doghouse, next to Brownie and the most recent litter of pot hound pups she had produced that year. The next morning after he left for work, I went inside, got dressed, and headed off to school. To show him that I had learned my lesson, I stayed in my school uniform until he returned that evening. Many hours had already passed, and I was hoping that he would have been satisfied with the punishment that he had already inflicted. However, I was mistaken for as soon as he entered the house, he grabbed my arm and continued from where he had left off. It seemed like there was no break between the current beating and the one I had received the night before. This time, because I dared to escape, the severity of the beating was amplified. He said that we had to understand the importance of education.

Even after all these years, the memory of that beating still lies deep beneath the scar tissue of my many life experiences. As I reflected on my childhood, memories of numerous youthful indiscretions flooded my mind. However, whenever I took my daughter to the Hollows or anywhere in the vicinity of the Queen's Park Savannah, that memory would bubble up to the surface. While I deserved to be disciplined for truancy, with the benefit of hindsight, what I was subjected to was nothing short of child abuse. Much like my teacher, he too grew up under colonial domination and would have received his share of blows. His notion of discipline, therefore, was to perpetuate the cycle of oppression, unaware of the damage being inflicted. I didn't know that then, but I know it now.

The Emperor Valley Zoo, lying adjacent to the Botanical Gardens were regular stops on our Sunday morning jaunts.

Strolling through the zoo with my daughter brought back even more memories of my youthful misadventures. Like the Sunday morning when my brother and I were sent to church. Instead of attending mass as instructed, we made a detour and ended up at the zoo. Our plan was to remain there and be home around the time the service would be over. The zoo was not yet opened to the public when we arrived, and there was no security to deter us from illegally entering. The fact that the gate was closed was not even a deterrent. We climbed the barbed wire fence and headed to the area where the turtles were kept. The sight of hundreds of young turtles crawling in every direction was something to behold. They were too beautiful to simply admire, I had to have one for myself. Casting aside the possible consequences, I grabbed a young turtle and tucked it under my white shirt. Trying not to arouse suspicion, we walked briskly towards the fence where we had entered, with the fear of being caught intensifying with every step. No longer able to control our emotions, we broke into a sprint that would have made Usain Bolt proud. While fleeing the scene of the crime, my pants got caught in the barbed wire fence. I felt a burning sensation between my legs but did not stop to investigate. Sprinting all the way, we arrived home with the turtle in hand and my pants in tatters with blood running down my legs. Under intense questioning by my parents, the truth about how we acquired the turtle was quickly revealed. Between my brother and me, we could not come up with a plausible alibi to hide our crime. Consequently, we both received a severe beating for not going to church, stealing, and destroying my good pants.

These memories flooded my mind whenever I visited the area with my daughter. I would tell her these stories with such drama and animation, that although she had no idea what I was saying, she would laugh uncontrollably, loving the dramatic re-enactment of my childhood misadventures. Recounting these tales, I found solace in her laughter, a balm for old wounds.

Amidst the turmoil of separation and the physical distance that separated us, thoughts of my children kept me grounded. While we were separated by vast distances across land and sea, thinking about them kept my heart warm and somehow shortened the distance. I wrote letters, sent postcards, and phoned with such regularity, that it would have been financially prudent to purchase a ticket to visit them in person. When the pain of separation was most severe, I often considered surrendering the dream and returning to the island. I could have had my old job back or resumed my career with another insurance company. My impressive track record was documented, and my name was recognized in the industry. The company's statistics consistently ranked me among the top producers in the Caribbean and the Americas. Given my history of accomplishment, I believe that my previous company or a competitor would have hired me in a heartbeat. But, instead of allowing myself to be consumed and swayed by emotions, I chose to continue the journey, knowing that this too shall pass.

I've never regretted leaving the island, but every now and then I would reflect on the life I left behind and the possibility of becoming another big fish in that small pond. Like the deluded emperor in his new clothes, I would have continued to live in relative comfort with a misguided sense of importance. Having lived on the island for almost 30 years, I was intimately familiar with the culture, the people, and their way of life. There were times when I missed the carefree lifestyle and the gay abandon that is the hallmark of the Trinidad carnival celebration and similar public events that injects life into the city. I often thought about the revellers on J'ouvert morning, filtering out of fetes exhausted and intoxicated. With women in front and men holding them from behind, exerting just enough energy to chip to the beat of the music, in the cool hours of the morning. The images of masqueraders covered in grease, mud, and talcum powder often placed me in a state of nostalgia. I miss standing on the bank of the Las Quevas River, watching hastily constructed watercrafts of questionable quality, held together with rope and discarded materials, race each other for nautical supremacy. Fuelled by copious amounts of weed and alcohol, I would laugh as they struggled to keep their vessels afloat, while caldrons of food bubbled on the riverbank. Inevitably, these hastily constructed floating contraptions would sink to the bottom, forcing the hapless crew to swim to shore. I missed the fete matches in Carenage and Macqueripe and beach limes on Maracas Bay, where drinks flowed, and the tantalizing aroma of spice-filled foods wafted in the breeze, competing for airspace with the pulsating rhythms of soca music and calypso. However, as fun, and as exciting as these social events were, I knew that despite its tropical charm, the world was much bigger than this little paradise in the south-eastern corner of the Caribbean that many say is the best country in the world. So, to maintain my focussed, I often thought of what my life and that of my siblings would have been like, if my mother had abandoned her dream for a better life in Trinidad. It was a question for which I have no answer. As I reminisced about the vibrant culture of my homeland, feeling pangs of nostalgia for its lively festivals and carefree spirit, I knew that my aspirations extended beyond the confines of my tropical paradise. So, with a heavy heart and unwavering determination, I forged ahead, trusting that time would heal the wounds of the past and pave the way for a brighter tomorrow.

Drama on the High Sea

Reflecting on the impending impact of immigration on my family, memories flooded back of my mother's journey nearly thirty years prior. In an era where Britain and North America enticed Caribbean islanders, with numerous employment opportunities, it was not uncommon for people to leave the Caribbean islands to venture abroad. For several years these Governments had been actively recruiting people from the colonies to do the work that their white citizens refused to perform, and people took advantage of the opportunity to immigrate. Many of these islands were British colonies, and Britain was referred to as the mother country. Like many colonialized people from across the empire, my mother could have gone to Britain to work as a domestic. Instead, she had left Grenada, entrusting her four children to her aunt's care, seeking opportunity in Trinidad.

Affectionately referred to as the Isle of Spice, Grenada is a small island in the Southern Caribbean with a surface area of 344 square kilometres. Despite its minute size, it is the world's biggest exporter of nutmeg and mace crops, spices that are increasingly in demand by the food industry on account of their flavouring qualities. Grenada boasted tropical charm consisting of, lush vegetation, crystal clear water, white sand beaches and fertile lands, yet the allure of Trinidad's prosperity beckoned. Employment opportunities for herself and education for her children, were all available in Trinidad, the fifth largest and most prosperous island in the Caribbean. With a land surface area of approximately 4,748 square kilometres, Trinidad was a step up, a new horizon even in terms of geography.

When my mother departed for Trinidad, I was just a toddler still in diapers. Because of my tender age at the time, I cannot say for how long she had been gone, but it was certainly long enough for her to fade from my memory. Years later, I learned that on the day she returned, I was playing in the yard. Delighted to see her baby again, she ran towards me with open arms. As far as I knew, I had never seen this woman before, so I ran into the house screaming. "Ah, lady!" "Ah, lady." The child to whom she had given birth and sustenance from her large breast that had fed so many before me, had no recollection of her. Broken hearted and devastated, she sat in the yard, under the shade of a mango tree weeping inconsolably, while her aunt tried to comfort her but to no avail.

Shortly after she returned, we set sail for Trinidad, embarking on a voyage toward a new beginning. Little did we know, fate had more in store. The year was 1958, and she was a young mother in her early 30s with four children for whom she was solely responsible. Chalice, the eldest of my siblings, was eight years old, and a two-year gap separated one succeeding sibling from the other in descending order. I was the baby of the De Gale clan when we embarked on that journey but, my position in the family structure would undergo a dramatic change before we arrived at our destination. My mother was pregnant when we boarded the vessel on our way to Trinidad. Based on her calculations, she should have been due a few weeks after arriving in our adopted country. Notwithstanding the occasional hurricane, this journey by sea was usually routine and uneventful. However, while on board, my mother went into labor amidst the turbulent waters of the Caribbean. In a scene worthy of a Hollywood medical drama, she was about to give birth to her fifth child on the open sea, somewhere between the islands of Trinidad and Grenada. Unsurprisingly, the vessel was not equipped for such emergencies, and neither was there any medical personnel on board among the passengers or crew to lend a helping hand. Its main function was to ferry passengers and cargo from one island to the other. After several turbulent hours at sea, the boat finally arrived at the Port of Spain harbour, and medical personnel on the island were immediately summoned. As curious onlookers gathered to witness the commotion, an ambulance arrived on the scene in highly dramatic fashion. With sirens blaring and emergency lights flashing, she was scurried away just in the nick of time, so that my brother could make his debut at the Port of Spain General Hospital, a testament to my mother's resilience. Mau was the first of my siblings to be born in Trinidad. Over the next eight years, four more children would follow at two-year intervals, leaving just enough space in-between for each of us to breathe.

Arriving in Trinidad, we found ourselves adrift, until our stepfather unknown to us at the time, stepped forward, guiding us to safety. Amidst the upheaval, we forged bonds that would shape our futures. I was two years old when we landed on the island, and for the next 28 years, Trinidad was the only home that I had ever known. For nearly three decades, Trinidad was our sanctuary, shaping my identity and echoing my mother's journey. Like the tectonic plates whose friction forced these islands to rise out of the sea, it was here that I became aware of myself and the numerous forces that moulded me for better or for worse. As I approached the age she was when she immigrated, I couldn't help but ponder the echoes of history. By some historical coincidence and in several significant ways, the trajectory of my life parallels that of my mother's. Like me, my mother had just turned thirty when she immigrated to Trinidad while I and some of my siblings were as young as my children were when I left them on the island. I thought about how I had forgotten my own mother and wondered if my children would forget me as I had forgotten her so many years ago. History was about to repeat itself and the thought of my children not knowing who I am was devastating. Determined not to repeat the past, I resolved to reunite my family before time eroded our connection. Just as my mother braved the unknown for us, I would do whatever it takes to ensure our bond endures while trying not to get lost in the mists of time, like my mother before me.

Growing Up on the Island

Growing up on the island was a journey defined by resourcefulness within the constraints of limited finances, a microcosm of the larger community in which we lived. While our humble household mirrored the broader community, unlike stereotypical portrayals, crime and gangs were alien concepts to us. Despite our weak economic standing, poverty served as a unifying force, though its depth often eluded us. However, it was nothing compared to what Frank McCourt called "a different class" in his book, Angela's Ashes. We lacked the awareness of the socio-political factors shaping our circumstances, viewing wealth as a simple contradiction. The nuances of historical injustices like slavery and colonialism were watered down in our education, fostering a belief in the meritocratic myth of hard work leading to prosperity. To us it was simple, some people were rich, and some were poor. Occasional access to movies, books, and newspapers gave us a peek into the lives of people living in luxury. We never questioned our status nor asked why rich people were mostly of the Caucasian persuasion. Our education did not prepare us to understand the impact of slavery and colonialism. Instead, we grew up with the often-mistaken belief that if you work hard and pull yourself up by the bootstraps, you too could live a life of luxury. But poor people are some of the hardest working people to be found anywhere in the world. In fact, no one worked harder than enslaved people and despite their efforts, they, like us often had no boots and, therefore, no straps with which to pull ourselves up, neither literally nor figuratively.

People worked hard and our community thrived on mutual support, evident in neighbors banding together during times of need. Disputes, albeit fleeting, centered around mundane issues like property boundaries and misbehaving children. Yet, no quarrel was so intractable that it could not be amicably resolved. Poverty spurred innovation; adults devised means to provide for their families while children crafted imaginative pastimes. With no access to credit, one way to generate a lump sum was through an informal banking system known as Sou Sou. Sou Sou offered a lifeline, pooling resources to alleviate financial burdens. Once a week, members would contribute a fixed amount into a pool. Then at the end of each month, one member would receive the entire sum, until every everyone received his or her "Hand." If another group were able to make the financial commitment, the pool would start over again. Having access to a lump sum of money, enabled participants to make purchases that would otherwise be unattainable if one depended solely on earned income.

Despite financial hardships, we were fortunate to have access to sustenance through our land. We planted a variety of fruits and vegetables such as plums, mangoes, tomatoes, lettuce, peas, corn, string beans, peppers, carrots, yams, and dasheen. Livestock, and crops, ranging from chickens to cassava and a goat name Meg, provided the protein for our daily sustenance. Cassava root was grounded in a hand-operated mill as part of the process. Milk, sugar, vanilla essence, nutmeg, and other ingredients were added to create the delicious cassava pone. Ground provision and green bananas were prepared with salt fish, okra, onions, and tomatoes with a dash of vegetable oil, creating an amazing dish. These foods were essential to our survival and featured prominently in our daily diet.

Since root vegetables require a constant supply of water, often in short supply, our resourcefulness extended to devising an irrigation system that ensured a steady supply of water for crops even in times of scarcity. This innovation made it possible to have an abundance of crops throughout the year, each in their own season. Rainwater collected in barrels was also used for bathing, washing, and feeding the animals. Rainwater harvesting and the installation of a massive water tank alleviated our dependence on public utilities. Before leaving for school every morning, we watered the plants, fed the animals, swept the yard, and tied Meg in a field to graze.

The bounty of our land went beyond mere sustenance; it was intertwined with cultural significance. The lush foliage of dasheen, tanya, and other ground provisions grew in abundance. Young dasheen leaves were used to make calaloo soup or served as a side dish to be eaten with rice, stewed chicken, beef, or pork. Dasheen and tanya leaves are nutritious food sources for human consumption, but spiders also benefit from their versatility. On the underside of these leaves, spiders wove intricate webs, capturing mosquitoes, and other small insects, and wrapping prey tightly in silk for future consumption, offering a mesmerizing display of nature's ingenuity. In Earl Lovelace's play, "The Dragon Can't Dance"

Aldrick the dragon maker says to Sylvia, the beautiful young virgin,

"Yuh skin smooth like de underside of ah Tanya leaf."

Anyone who has ever seen the underside of the dasheen or tanya leaf would appreciate the pure poetry in this most Caribbean of compliment, referencing its unique color and silky texture. In addition to being death traps for unsuspecting prey, spider webs also capture raindrops that sparkle like diamonds when sunlight is refracted. The compelling beauty of these leaves could rival that of any rose while having the added advantage of being edible, delicious, and highly nutritious.

In the tapestry of island life, our upbringing was colored by resilience, community bonds, and the innate ability to find beauty and sustenance amidst scarcity. In our backyard, stood a majestic breadfruit tree, its expansive leaves matching the grandeur of its fruit. We utilized the breadfruit in various culinary creations, such as roasting, frying, or simmering it with coconut milk, salted pigtails, scotch bonnet peppers, and an array of spices to craft the delectable Oil Down. Our backyard was a bounty of fruits and vegetables, including mangoes, coconuts, plums, and the prolific soursop, whose prickly exterior concealed juicy white flesh. Soursop juice was transformed with additions like milk, nutmeg, cinnamon, sugar, and vanilla essence into a refreshing and nutritious beverage. Freezing some of the juice into ice blocks provided relief from the mid-day heat, as we playfully let the melting juice trickle down our arms, savoring its delectable taste before it could fall to the ground.

Among the harvest, bananas were the most abundant, providing ample supply for banana bread and cakes. Our sustenance predominantly came from the fertile land provided by nature. However, acquiring manufactured goods like clothes and shoes was a challenge due to financial constraints. This often led to playful anecdotes when one was not wearing underwear. Rather than admit the truth, we would claim in jest, that the pants and underwear were torn in the same spot.

Our livestock primarily consisted of chickens, ducks, turkeys, and a goat named Meg. Chicken furnished the main protein for our meals. Yet, before reaching the dinner table, the chicken underwent a process of capture, decapitation, and scalding to remove feathers. Occasionally, a headless fowl would escape our grasp, causing a mix of terror and amusement among us children. The chicken would complete a few laps around the yard before it would collapse or be restrained.

At the age of five or six years old, I was playing in the yard when a teenage boy threw a corn cob that accidentally connected with my family jewels. Startled, he fled quickly as I lay on the ground in pain. The next day, my penis was severely infected, leading to a hospital admission. Visiting hours had not officially begun when my mother came to visit. However, because my bed was located close to the veranda, we were able to communicate. With a gentle smile on her face, she lovingly inquired about my well-being.

" How yuh feelin?" she asked.

"Good," I replied innocently, delighted to see her.

" Wha de doctor do?" she asked lovingly.

"Noting," I responded.

Noticing a bulge in my diaper, she inquired, " What yuh have dere?"

"Noting," I replied, unaware of the surgery I had undergone.

" Pull dong yuh diaper leh meh see," she requested.

Without hesitation, I complied and was surprised to find my penis wrapped in bandages. Before panic could set in, she assured me,

" Everyting go be awright, de doctor do someting to make yuh feel better."

Her comforting words eased my worry, and when she handed me a lollipop, I promptly forgot the issue. A few years later, an older boy called me a Jew before running off with laughter echoing behind him. Confused, I recounted the incident to my brother, who was two years older and mature beyond his years.

" Doh worry bout dat," he said. "Jesus was a Jew too."

Still puzzled, I asked what Jesus had to do with the boy's comment about my genitals.

"Jesus was circumcised too, just like you," he explained.

My brother's reassurance that I was in good company eased my mind. Although the surgery had been performed years before the boy's comment, it was only then that I understood the medical procedure I had undergone. Thereafter, I was no longer bothered by the remark, and as an adult, I am quite pleased with the result. It is very hygienic, resembles my head, and on a more personal note, women who know have often referred to it as handsome.

Adventures and Tragedies

My stepfather worked as a carpenter on the Trinidad National Flour Mill during the period of its construction. Although he had never been a carpenter's apprentice, he was highly competent with tools. The trade came to him by way of observation but mostly through osmosis. One fateful day, while atop the mill's roof, he plummeted over 30 feet to the ground, saved only by a mound of loose dirt that softened his landing. Although he survived, the fall left him with a debilitating back injury, requiring him to use a brace whenever the pain became unbearable. Thankfully he survived the fall for as one of the main breadwinners in the household, his death would have dealt a devastating blow to our family. Moreover, without funds for a burial, the irony of the dirt that saved him potentially becoming his grave was not lost on us.

The flour mill, situated over 10 km from our home in Belmont, was a central feature of our childhood adventures. It was built on the sea bank, and water that was used to cool the machinery inside was pumped into the sea twenty-four hours a day, seven days a week. This constant expulsion of hot wastewater agitated the seabed, minimizing visibility and raising the water temperature to a comfortable level. The area was also a dumping ground for barges that were no longer sea-worthy and the preferred habitat for various sea-dwelling creatures, most notably jellyfish. Despite the many wrecks that littered the seabed, it was an ideal location for kids on summer vacation in search of adventure. During August holidays, we'd trek to the mill to swim in the warm murky waters. This was our playground, where we'd spend entire summer days swimming, always careful to return home before our parents.

During our escapades, I often observed a small boy of East Indian descent, showcasing his swimming prowess with daring dives off partly submerged barges. We were roughly the same age, and although he was smaller in stature, he was undoubtedly an excellent swimmer. I know now that his physical stature had nothing to do with his ability to swim, but in my young mind, it was a justifying factor. He would climb to the top of one of the barges, summersault into the water, and resurface, repeating the manoeuvre time and again. Aware that he was being observed, his antics became even more performative. After witnessing the ease with which he executed his manoeuvres, I was convinced of my own ability to perform in an aquatic environment. Prior to that day, I always stayed close to the shore, never venturing any further than waist-deep in seawater. Nevertheless, his fearlessness inspired me to extend my boundaries beyond it's normal limits. Bolstered by false confidence, I decided that since he was smaller than me, there was no reason why I could not swim in the deep. Taking nothing else into consideration, I summoned the courage, climbed to the highest point of the partly submerged barge, and dove into the water. The dive was well executed, but when I returned to the surface and realized that my feet could no longer touch the ground, I panicked. In desperation, I splashed towards another barge, secured to the dock by a thick rope. With my heart racing frantically, I grabbed the rope and pulled myself onto the barge. The rope was attached to the dock, and I could have used it to pull myself ashore. However, paralyzed by fear, I could not muster the courage to enter the water again. From my perch on the barge, the shore seemed much further away than usual. Marooned, I sat there awaiting rescue, like a castaway on a desert island.

Hours passed without my friends realizing that I was in a pickle. When it was time to go, they called out, leaving me with no choice but to inform them of my plight. A man who also happened to be swimming in the area came to my aid. After much persuasion, I climbed on his back and immediately placed him in a chokehold, a desperate reaction to paralyzing panic. It was his physical strength and swimming ability that averted tragedy beneath the waves that day.

Despite this harrowing experience, I persisted, eventually learning to swim by holding the rope, letting go at intervals and threading water until I finally got the hang of it. However, not all tales from those treacherous waters were triumphant. Soon after conquering my fear of the deep, a boy around the age of twelve attempted the same manoeuvre and disappeared beneath the water. When he failed to resurface, his younger brother sheepishly informed us of what had happened. As a recently minted swimmer, I was excited to join the search party. Although it was impossible to see more than a few inches beneath the surface, my excitement was palpable. For me, this was the ultimate adventure, a quest to retrieve a drowned soul from its watery grave. We were combing the area where the boy had disappeared, returning to the surface for air and diving down again to continue the search. It was on one of these return dives that I came face to face with him lying on the seabed with his eyes wide open. The sight of the boy's lifeless body beneath the murky water scared me half to death. Instead of grabbing hold of him, I raced to the surface in a frantic attempt to put some distance between myself and the boy's dead body. Swallowing copious amounts of warm salt water, I raced towards the shore, shouting,

"Ah see em! Ah see em!"

The older and more experienced swimmers immediately converged on the area and his body was recovered close to where I had indicated. From the shore, I watched as they dragged his lifeless corpse out of the water. That was the first time I had ever seen a dead person. What surprised me even more was that the body was that of a boy. I had always associated death with old people, and it never occurred to me that young people also die. News of the drowning spread quickly, and people gathered to witness the commotion. We gawked at his lifeless body lying on the beach in a pair of white underwear labelled "Fruit of the Loom." This was a spectacle that none of us had ever experienced. News of the drowning had reached his mother, and within half an hour, she arrived on the scene screaming hysterically.

"Steve!" she shouted.

"Oh God, Oh God, Steve!"

"Wake up, boy, get up!"

"Say somting boy, say somting!" But he was unresponsive.

"Jesus Christ, look at de cross I ha to bear dis mornin!"

"Oh God, Oh God! She cried. "Wake up, Steve, get up boy, wake up!"

She screamed his name repeatedly, hoping that he would open his eyes or that she would awake from what she must have been hoping was a bad dream. Squeezing him tightly against her voluptuous breast, salt water gushed from his mouth. This was the most heart-wrenching scene that any of us had ever witnessed in our young lives. Finally, the ambulance arrived to take him to the morgue while she was still rocking him like a baby in her arms. Long after the flashing emergency lights had faded in the distance, the sound of her voice continued to reverberate in my head.

Weeks later, summoning the courage, we returned to our favourite swimming spot, but nothing had changed. The warm wastewater that flowed from the flour mill still agitated the seabed, reducing visibility to zero. The area, a welcoming spot for adventurous young boys and a preferred habitat for jellyfish and various sea-dwelling creatures. The drowning of the boy and the subsequent retrieval from its watery grave, served only as a stark reminder of mortality's cruel reach. Yet, the allure remained, tempered only by the memory of a lost life, etched forever in the depths.

In the heat of August, despite the unsettling loss of a boy to drowning, our thirst for adventure remained unquenched. Just a stone's throw from the flour mill lay a swamp, where mangrove trees grew, their tangled roots protruding above the ground like alien life forms. Here, amidst the murky waters that were their natural habitat, blue crabs thrived. Rain would flood their subterranean homes, coaxing them to the surface in search of mates and sustenance. With claws raised high above their heads, hundreds of crabs would be roaming the swamp ready to engage in battle for food and sexual gratification. Sensing danger, they'd retreat underground until the coast was clear, often facing threats from birds, lizards, and the greatest menace of all: adventurous kids making the most of summer holidays. We'd plunge our arms into crab burrows, seizing them as they struggled, sometimes sacrificing limbs in their bid for freedom. Despite the occasional vice-like grip on our fingers, we persisted, these captured crustaceans becoming supplements to our Sunday meals, cooked in callaloo, and served with rice and meat. When not navigating murky waters or grappling with crabs, our days were filled with marbles, football, kite-flying, roller races, and cricket matches. These pastimes, heightened during the scorching summer months, consumed our days. On what was literally not a level playing field, we would play half-naked and shoeless from morning to night. The field sloped slightly to the south so that when it rained, water drained off immediately. With rocks jutted out all over the ground, we may as well have been playing on a minefield. In the heat of a football match, a player would inevitably stump his toe against a rock, dislodging the nail from its bed. Screaming in agony, he would fall to the ground, the game would stop for a moment, giving him time to exit the field and attend to his injury. Undeterred by the experience, the injured player would return a week or two later, with no apparent recollection of the incident. The possibility of sustaining injuries came with the territory, an integral part of our childhood experience. Despite the frequency of these injuries, we continued to do battle on that minefield, primarily because there were no officially designated areas for kids to play safely.

Our daily trek to and from primary school, spanning over 16 kilometers, morphed into a game and despite the distance travelled, we never felt tired. My brother and I would shoulder both school bags in turns, swapping at lampposts along the way, turning the mundane journey into a lighthearted game. Each of us would take turns carrying both school bags at once, alternating back and forth at every lamppost, so that at any given time, one of us would be walking hands-free. The spacing of the lampposts added to the fun. Some were close together while others were several meters apart. This meant that one of us would have to carry the bags for a much longer or shorter distance. Whether the switch was immediate or delayed, we would have a good laugh at the one who got stuck carrying the bags. But one day, we encountered a bully who held me hostage. In exchange for my freedom, he demanded that we hand over our lunch money. With no money to negotiate my freedom, my brother didn't hesitate to defend me, using a rock to thwart the assailant. The rock landed squarely on his chest, and as he staggered to retain his balance, we ran as fast as our feet would carry us. Fearful of retaliation, at the end of the school day we abandoned our regular path in favour of the much longer route.

Upon recounting the incident to our mother, she accompanied us to school the next day. Halfway into our commute, he emerged from behind a wall armed with a piece of wood. Unaware that the short Indian-looking woman behind us was our mother, he approached aggressively. As soon as we saw him, we both scampered to hide behind her. My mother was no more than five feet tall, and because the bully was a big kid, he towered over her. Showing no sign of fear, she stopped him in his tracks and gave him the most serious tongue lashing he may have ever received in his short criminal life. Scaring him half to death, she threatened to call the police if he ever bothered us again. Visibly shaken, he could hardly make eye contact with her. She relieved him of the piece of wood, made him apologize and promise never to harass us again, before abruptly dismissing him. Although our paths had crossed several times since then, her intervention quelled his harassment, ensuring our safety without further incident.

Parties beckoned us as teenagers, and regardless of our financial constraints, we found a way to attend. Pooling our meager resources, we purchase Ruby Rich, Gold Coin, or Charlie's Red Spanish wines, all of which were ideally priced to suit our trifling budget. Oblivious to their effects on our young bodies, after downing a bottle of wine before a party, I found myself in a dire bathroom predicament. It was after eleven when we arrived, and the party was in full swing. The house was packed to capacity, and the heat being generated made it feel like a sauna. The wine was having its intended effect when I broke into a cold sweat. First, there was a sharp pain in my stomach, followed by loud bubbling noises. The line to the washroom was long, and the need to go was extremely urgent. Any delay would have resulted in an accident on the dance floor. In desperation, I forced my way through the crowd and made a dash to the darkest corner of the backyard, just in time to squat. Within minutes, the bubbling in my stomach subsided and the cool morning air blowing gently on my face, made me feel alive again. With no access to paper, I resorted to using my socks. It was just after 1 a.m. when I returned to the party to get my friend.

"Leh we go," I intoned with a sense of urgency.

"Wah?" He responded, "Buh we jus reach here."

"Ah know," I replied, "But we ha to go now."

"Ah jus getting in de groove an ah marking something," he replied.

"Ah know, buh we ha to go," I insisted.

After all the effort that we had made to get to the fete, he wanted to know why I needed to leave so urgently, but I couldn't tell him while we were still at the party. We had been there for a relatively brief time, and after haranguing him for several more minutes, he finally capitulated. On the way home, I told him what had happened, and we both had a good laugh. Our hasty departure led to a ban on future parties at the host's home, courtesy of her father's discovery in the backyard.

Remembering Meg

On a vibrant Carnival Tuesday afternoon, amidst the pulsating rhythms of the parade, I laid eyes on the girl who would hold my heart captive. She was in a band with her sister while her overly protective father waited for them at an agreed-upon intersection. Her father loved carnival, and although he was extremely protective, he wanted his daughters to experience its magic, if only for a moment. The granting of that permission would alter the trajectory of my life and that of his favourite daughter forever. Dressed in a mustard-colored top and a pair of black pants, she exuded a magnetic charm that drew me in. For less than half an hour, I held her close to me, the intoxicating music intensifying the ecstasy. As we approached the intersection where her father was waiting dutifully, our brief connection amidst the revelry left me spellbound for as she left the band, the spirit of carnival followed quickly in lockstep. Deflated by her departure, I returned home long before the parade was over, not knowing her name nor how she could be contacted.

Weeks later, fate reunited us at an evening class, where our conversations blossomed. We chatted for a long time, and I always looked forward to seeing her whenever class was in session. On one occasion, the class held a picnic in The Hollows, and we spent the entire day together. I must have made a good impression, for she invited me to a bazaar that was being held at her high school. My house was situated close to the school that she attended, and our goat Meg was often tied on the school grounds to graze in the tall grass that defined the school's perimeter. However, there was one detail I kept hidden: my humble responsibility of goat herding.

Meg, a goat of the Saanen variety, the biggest of the dairy breeds was more than just livestock; she was a cherished member of our family. She was tall and milk-white with a goatee that hung to the middle of her chest. Meg's milk sustained us, providing both nourishment and sustenance. Yet, I hesitated to reveal this truth, mindful of the societal gap between us. Every morning, I or one of my brothers would take Meg to graze wherever the grass was tall and plentiful. At the end of the day, her udders would be filled, and she could be depended upon to deliver the protein we required to meet our daily needs. For Meg, every meal was a banquet. A prolific producer of milk for drinking and for making cheese, she was clearly an important source of food for our entire family.

On the day of the bazaar, I tied Meg on the perimeter of the schoolyard where the green grass laboured under the weight of the morning dew. We were still in the courting period of our relationship, and because Trinidad is a class-conscious society, I had no intention of revealing my goat herding activities. While my family had to wage a daily struggle just to keep our heads above water, hers was an aspiring middle-class family for whom life was comparatively easy. Her mother worked for the Government, and her father was a supervisor at an international mining company. They owned a house in an upwardly mobile neighbourhood, and her father drove her and her sisters to and from school. If his work schedule conflicted with his family obligations, he would hire a taxi to get them to school and back. He had four daughters, and the need to protect them from perceived ragamuffins like me must have turned him into the tyrant who struck fear in the hearts of young suitors. Without question, he was the undisputed head of his household and ruled it with an iron fist. Nevertheless, he loved his family unconditionally and would go to any length to protect them. So, given the social and economic disparity between us, I thought it was best not to mention that I was simply a goat herder.

We were strolling the school grounds when Meg's unexpected appearance threatened to expose my secret. She had escaped from where I had tied her that morning and was wandering the schoolyard when our eyes made four. Immediately, she recognized me and before I could react, she approached blurting out her familiar greeting, *meeeeeeeeeg, meeeeeeeg; meeeeeeg*. I tried to ignore her, but she was unrelenting. Then I tried to lose her in the crowd, but she refused to go away. Despite the hundreds of young people at the bazaar, the goat insisted on engaging with me, which peaked my girlfriend's curiosity, prompting her to ask,

"Michael, you know dis goat?"

"No," I replied, denying our shared history.

'Yuh sure yuh doh know dis goat? She look like she know you." She declared.

"I doh no way dis goat come from," I insisted.

Yet, guilt gnawed at me as Meg persisted in her pursuit.

Oblivious of the embarrassment that she had provoked, Meg continued to follow me. Not only did I know the goat, but I also owned it. Like the apostle Peter had denied Jesus, I denied knowing Meg. To escape further embarrassment, we retreated indoors as Meg continued to search for me. That evening Meg walked herself home while I waited with my girlfriend, ensuring to disappear just before her father would arrive. On my way home, I thought of Meg and felt badly about how I had denied knowing her. She had been an important part of our family since she was a kid, and we had played with her and the many kids that she had produced over the years. I should have said,

"Yes, this is my goat," but I could not bring myself to admit that simple truth.

I don' know what difference it would have made, but I was afraid I might lose her. Meg was munching on the grass that had been gathered for her dinner when I returned home that evening.

I said, "Meg, ah see yuh make it home by yuhself."

She lifted her head, looked at me with her big brown eyes, put her head down, and continued eating, a clear indication that Meg did not take rejection lightly.

Weeks later, tragedy struck. I had tied Meg to a tree on an embankment in the schoolyard where the tall grass was bending like an arc under the weight of the rain that had fallen overnight. The sun was struggling to break through the overcast sky and the cool, grey morning had an eerie feeling that Meg must have sensed. Although this was a routine with which she was familiar, her behaviour was uncharacteristically restless. Despite her uneasiness, I tied her on the embankment near the school, where the grass was green, tall, and plentiful. At the end of the day, her udders would be filled with the milk we needed to meet our daily requirements. However, when I went to retrieve her that evening, Meg was nowhere to be found. My first thoughts were that she had escaped or that someone had stolen her. But, as I got closer, I noticed the rope that was used to secure her was still attached to the tree. My heart sank when I looked over the embankment and saw Meg hanging off the side of the cliff with the rope pulled tightly around her neck and her tongue hanging loosely on the side of her mouth. I knew in an instant that Meg was dead.

"How yuh could be so schupid to tie she on de bank?" I asked myself.

I wondered if my refusal to acknowledge her a few weeks earlier may have contributed to her untimely demise, but there was no way of knowing.

Guilt and grief consumed me as I grappled with the consequences of my actions. Had my denial led to Meg's demise? I wondered.

Meg's passing cast a shadow over our family, her absence a palpable loss. Yet, in the face of hardship, my stepfather, pragmatic yet compassionate, ensured Meg's legacy lived on. Her sacrifice provided sustenance for weeks to come.

In the ensuing years, the girl from the band became my wife and the mother of my children, a testament to the unpredictable twists of fate. And though Meg was gone, her memory remained etched in our hearts, a poignant reminder of the fragility of life and the depth of human connections.

The Price of Admission

At the age of eighteen, my mother faced a harsh reality: the loss of her mother, leaving her and her younger sister to fend for themselves. With her father's absence shrouded in mystery, my maternal lineage remained a blank page. Born circa 1924, she never advanced past elementary school, navigating a world where education held little sway for girls from the lower echelons of society. Yet, she often remarked that wisdom trumped over books, evident in her common sense and knowledge that seemed to rival a Ph.D. Despite her limited formal education, she understood from personal experience in the school of hard knocks, the pivotal role education played in societal and economic advancement. Thus, she resolved to afford her children more opportunities than fate had bestowed upon her.

Unwittingly, I became her scribe shortly after acquiring the written word. Her dictations became my reluctant chore, though she often had to keep my wandering mind in check. Failing the Common Entrance Examination (GCE) dimmed my prospects of entering secondary school for a free education. Yet, my mother perceived potential beyond my exam scores. Over the years that I had reluctantly written her letters, she must have seen something in me that I had not yet seen in myself, a belief that sustained her as she negotiated my enrollment with the high school principal.

Behind closed doors, they agreed that a sum of forty dollars would secure my admission. Forty dollars is little more than a pittance now, but for a parent struggling to raise eight children, it was nothing short of a king's ransom at the time. The bribe was to be paid in instalments and week after week, I dutifully delivered installments of this pact, burdened by a secret transaction that tainted my youthful conscience. I was not aware of it at the time, but bribery was rampant in every stratum of society and schools were no exception. However, the sacrifice that my mother had made on my behalf, inadvertently placed a heavy burden on my slender shoulders. Whenever I had to seek out the principal to deliver the envelope, my awareness of the agreement was a constant source of embarrassment. Otherwise, I made every effort to avoid him and could never look him in the eyes. In my young mind, I believed that whenever he saw me, he was reminded that my mother had bribed him so that I could attend his school. That may have been the last thing on his mind, but it was always front on mine. As a result, I felt inadequate and undeserving as if I did not belong, a condition now referred to as Imposter Syndrome. For my first two years in high school, I shouldered that heavy burden until one morning, we were ordered to remain assembled in the schoolyard. Although assembly was a daily occurrence, there was something different about this one. Teachers were running back, and forth, which caused the assembly to be delayed for much longer than normal. Instead of the muted mumbling that would normally be emanating from the student body, there was absolute silence. The air was thick with anticipation, and we had a premonition that something terrible had happened. We were becoming restless when the Vice-principal finally announced that the principal had died over the weekend. With this announcement, the entire student body responded with a collective gasp, shock, and disbelief. I too reacted, not with grief nor shock nor disbelief, but with an overwhelming sense of relief. It was as if a tremendous burden had been lifted from my shoulders; a burden of guilt that I no longer had to bear. The principal had died and would be buried with my secret. After holding my breath for two consecutive years, I was finally able to exhale. No longer encumbered by guilt, my mother's investment in me could still be realized, and she might finally get value her money.

After he had passed away, I thought about the situation that caused me such discomfort and how his untimely death allowed me to lay that burden down. He may also have felt uneasy whenever he saw me, because I knew about the bribe that he had taken from my mother. Reflecting on my discomfort, I pondered the prevalence of such transactions, wondering how many youths languished in ignorance due to financial barriers. I wondered how many other parents had to bribe school principals so that their children could have a shot at a high school education. More importantly, I wondered how many young people with tremendous potential would never see the inside of a high school classroom because their parents were unable to afford the price of admission. Whether it was greed or a desire to help a black kid for a price I cannot say. However, regardless of his personal motivation, I embraced the opportunity his decision afforded me, grateful for the chance to pursue an education. Despite his corrupt practice, may his soul rest in peace.

My mother had sacrificed for me to attend secondary school, but the quality of that education left much to be desired. From primary through secondary schools, I encountered teachers that should never have set foot in any classroom in a teaching capacity. Their communication skills were poor to say the least, and their knowledge of the subject matter left much to be desired. My Form 5 Math teacher for example, was the epitome of incompetence. He would spend the entire period talking about his family and how difficult it was to provide for them on his meagre salary. He once asked the class if anyone had family at Nestle that could get him a deal on baby formula. A few minutes before the period ended, he would solve one problem on the blackboard and tell us to study the next chapter. The following day he would do it all over again. It was as if every day of the entire term was Groundhog Day. We never complained because listening to him talk about his struggles was entertaining. Although we were aware that he was squandering our time, no one ever objected because he was the authority figure in the classroom. It is not surprising therefore, that so many of us struggled with math and other subjects. In addition to whatever issues students may have been dealing with, teachers like him made it even more difficult for us to excel academically.

The highest grade I ever received in math as a Form 5 student was forty-five out of one hundred percent. This grade was sufficient to place me at the top of the heap. This spoke to the quality of education we received and while I was happy to be ahead of my peers, I was also keenly aware that my performance was abysmal and found it difficult to relish in my so-called achievement. Despite my efforts, academic success remained elusive, until I encountered Mr. Adolphus Daniel.

Mr. Daniel's after-school program was a sanctuary for aspiring scholars, his unconventional teaching style breathing life into the classroom. His passion for education, coupled with his inspiring demeanor, ignited a fervor for learning among his students. Under his guidance, I flourished, achieving academic feats once deemed impossible. Despite not having access to a lab, he taught Math, Physics, and Chemistry on evenings and weekends. Mr. Daniel was a consummate professional with a teaching style that should be a model for all who aspire to a profession in education.

It was the 1970s, and the Black Power Revolution had ignited the consciousness of black youth. As young adults in the African diaspora, we were encouraged to embrace our history. In the classroom, Mr. Daniel was our role model. He inspired us, and we did our best to impress and emulate him. He had an Afro hairstyle and wore Dashiki shirts with a thick, heavy silver bracelet with clenched fists at both ends. An impassioned and outstanding communicator, Mr. Daniel was a young, gifted teacher with an unconventional style. He transformed the classroom into a theatre with him as the star of a one-man show. His passion for teaching, his resonant voice and his imposing physical frame all worked together to drive home the lessons. His was a theatrical performance that held us spellbound and left us clinging to every word that issued from his lips. His classes were filled with students who were struggling with the sciences but were eager to learn. He believed, respected, and encouraged us, and we responded enthusiastically. To ensure that we were not left behind, many of us would routinely do more homework than he had assigned. When my parents could not afford the fee, he allowed me to take the classes free of charge. I wouldn't be surprised if he extended that courtesy to other students as well.

At the end of the year, he hosted a Christmas dinner for his students at the Trinidad Hilton, which he must have heavily subsidized. We were poor kids, most of whom had never been to a restaurant, much less the Trinidad Hilton hotel. He made us feel that we mattered, and we made every effort not to disappoint him. When the General Certificate Examination (GCE) results were announced, 99% of the students he taught were successful. I received a distinction in Mathematics, a feat that would have previously been impossible to imagine. Mr. Daniel positively impacted the lives of thousands of students who had the privilege of studying under him. His impact on my life is still evident in the way I deliver presentations today. His impact extended far beyond the classroom, shaping the trajectories of countless lives. His legacy, though unsung, deserves recognition for its profound influence on generations of students. As I bid farewell to this remarkable educator, I take solace in the belief that his spirit stands among the revered ancestors, his contributions immortalized in the hearts of those he touched.

Upon completing five arduous years at Belmont Boys Secondary School, the momentous occasion of graduation finally arrived. In a peculiar collaboration, our school joined forces with Providence Girls, though the rationale behind it remained a mystery to us. Among our cohort, one stood out: Bob, a boy destined for greatness despite his diminutive stature and peculiar appearance—a multi-sided head perched atop his slender frame. Bob's academic brilliance made him a natural contender for valedictorian. Yet, his rapid speech pattern, posed a challenge for comprehension. While his intellect shone, my strength lay in the resonance of my voice and my adeptness in reading.

Assigned to read a passage from the Bible, Bob's haste left the overseeing nun unimpressed. Seizing the opportunity, she entrusted the task to me, and my delivery captured her attention. Thus, I was anointed as the valedictorian, though the prospect of crafting a speech from scratch daunted me. Drawing inspiration from Malcolm X's Autobiography, I composed a fervent address, much to the concern of our English teacher, Mr. Hazel. Advising caution, he offered to temper its radicalism, but I remained resolute in my vision.

At the ceremony's climax, emboldened by the call for Black empowerment, I delivered a stirring indictment of conformity, with the passion of Malcolm X, imploring my fellow graduates to resist the urge to become rubber stamps.

"...Conformity," I declared, "That refuge of the frightened is only a word, don't make it your reality...."

The response was overwhelming—an outpouring of applause and accolades from peers and faculty alike. Post-ceremony, the nun recognized my radio-worthy voice, offering an introduction to the local station manager. I had just turned eighteen, and although I knew nothing about the radio business, I answered in the affirmative. She said that she knew the station manager and would arrange an interview for me. With no further information, she went ahead and scheduled the appointment. A few days later, I was at the station manager's office. Prior to this, I had never been in a professional work environment for a job interview or for any reason whatsoever. Navigating the unfamiliar terrain of a professional setting, I found myself at the radio station, grappling with nerves and uncertainty. Although Belmont is less than half an hour north of the capital, I had never gone into Port of Spain nor visited any place of employment. Fifteen minutes later, he called me into his office, introduced himself and inquired about the job I was seeking. Without any hesitation, I replied,

"Anything."

I may have had the voice that could be trained for radio, but I certainly did not have the confidence, maturity, or intellectual capacity to be a Radio Announcer at the time. Furthermore, I had no idea about what transpires behind the scenes at radio stations and felt like I was in over my head. Though my voice held promise for radio, my lack of experience left me ill-prepared for the role of announcer. The interview concluded swiftly, leaving me grateful for the reprieve, as it became evident that my current abilities did not align with the demands of the position.

Reflecting on the encounter, it seemed the station manager, perhaps prompted by the nun's recommendation, extended the opportunity out of courtesy rather than genuine intent to hire. While the prospect of an apprenticeship might have nurtured any potential seen in me, the swift conclusion of the interview signaled a clear mismatch. Despite the setback, I harbored no regrets, relieved to return to the path of exploration and self-discovery beyond the confines of the interview room.

Making my Way

Upon completing high school, I made a solemn vow to never set foot in a classroom again. At just eighteen, the prospect of university seemed beyond reach, both financially and intellectually. Raised in a modest household, the idea of further education appeared unattainable, and I convinced myself it wasn't meant for someone like me. University wasn't part of the narrative in my circle; completing high school was the pinnacle of achievement. With that in mind, I eagerly sought my place in the workforce.

Back then, a high school diploma was more than enough to secure employment. I sent out applications while temporarily working at a family friend's convenience store in the city. However, a moment of embarrassment led me to abruptly quit, a decision fueled by youthful pride. I was sweeping the pavement in front of the shop when I looked up and saw a girl that I had a crush on in high school. She was in the company of her friends, laughing and talking as they advanced towards me. The thought of her seeing me performing such a menial task overwhelmed my sensibilities and without hesitation, I ran into the store and promptly quit. That was the first bridge that I had burned. In the ensuing years, several more would be reduced to ashes as I tried to navigate the world of work.

One of my earliest experiences, exposed me to the realities of labor and excess. I found myself apprenticing as a technician for a company servicing air conditioning and refrigeration units, both on land and offshore. My first assignment was on an oil rig, a few miles off the coast of the island. My brother had worked on one of these rigs before and often spoke about the thrill of riding in a helicopter. It was now my turn to experience the ride and I was looking forward to the thrill. The chopper arrived early to take us to the rig, and I had to make a concerted effort to curb my enthusiasm. Soon we were flying over the Caribbean Sea, an aquatic playground where dolphins were leaping out of the water and racing around like children at play. Within an hour after take-off, we arrived at our destination and were invited to join the crew for a buffet-style breakfast. There were over one hundred able-bodied men on the platform and food was prepared for the entire workforce. Eggs, bacon, ham, sausages, bread, pancakes, fruit, and an assortment of hot and cold drinks were available for consumption. I had never seen so much food in my entire life. The very sight of this gastronomic display left me famished and eager to put a significant dent in the offering. Like most eighteen-year-olds, I had an enormous appetite and a well-oiled metabolism that kept me under 120 pounds regardless of how much I consumed. My co-worker on the other hand, was a man of slightly less than average height in his mid to late forties. He weighed more than 280lbs, most of which was concentrated in his voluminous stomach. He often complained about the size of his stomach and his struggle to address the issue, but his weight proved to be a formidable opponent. I was still a growing boy who, in theory could have consumed an entire elephant without gaining an ounce. After serving myself a sample of everything that was on offer, I arrived at our table with a mountain of food on my plate. My partner, who had served himself a modest portion was astounded. I was the smallest and youngest person on the platform, and the men stared at me in amusement, thinking that my eyes were bigger than my stomach. To their surprise, I consumed every morsel of food and would have gone for seconds, had I not reminded myself that I was there to work not to eat. We were scheduled to remain on the oil rig overnight, and I was looking forward to lunch and dinner. The gods would have delighted in this banquet when lunch was finally revealed. There was chicken, steaks, beef, rice, potatoes, vegetables, and what seemed like every conceivable dessert. Again, my partner served himself another modest portion, but my plate was once more piled high. At dinner, I tried to be more discreet, but I couldn't resist the lamb and pork chops, and macaroni pie, and chicken, and veal, and mashed potatoes, among the other offerings. Given the quantity of food that lay before me, one would have assumed that my plate belonged to my partner and his belonged to me. Everything was in abundance, and although many mouths had been fed, there were tons of food leftover after dinner had ended. To my surprise, the food was thrown overboard, creating a feeding frenzy for the thousands of fish for whom every day was a banquet. The following day we were flown back to the island, and I was still trying to wrap my mind around the amount of food that was prepared and how much of it was thrown away. In as much as I enjoyed what I had consumed, I found the waste appalling. This left a lasting impression on my mind considering the number of people that went hungry in the city.

I stayed at this job for almost one year, during which time I travelled the length and breadth of the island servicing domestic and commercial units. The work was physically demanding and at the end of each day, I wore the evidence of a hardworking man. Since I always got a ride home after work, my generally dishevelled appearance was not much of a bother. One day, I was assigned to replace a fan belt in an industrial unit, not because of my technical expertise but rather, my slight physical frame. To accomplish this task, I had to wedge myself inside the cramped confines of the unit, which appeared not to have not been serviced for several years. Since joining the company, this was one of the dirtiest jobs that I had done. The unit was situated on the roof of a building in the heart of the city and when the job ended around the evening rush hour, I was covered in grease and grime. My partner had an appointment that day and was unable to drive me home. While waiting at the taxi stand in the company of other commuters, I became self-conscious and felt deeply embarrassed about my dishevelled appearance. I thought about the large number of industrial and domestic units we serviced, and the thousands of dollars that were generated daily by all its service technicians. Despite servicing dozens of units on any given day, my weekly salary was equivalent to servicing one window unit. To me, this was distressing. The next day I quit without notice. I wanted an office job with a desk and a telephone. Something with "an air of respectability" that did not involve physical labour.

Shortly after quitting that position, I landed a job as an Accounts Clerk with a company that sold jewellery and precious stones. This was my first office job that paid a monthly salary of $300 plus benefits. The job entailed monitoring inventory and ensuring that the accounts were balanced at the end of each day. To carry out my responsibilities, I was provided with a desk, a phone, and an electronic calculator. As far as I was concerned, I had made it. I learned the job quickly and understood the accounting process enough to function effectively on my own. After several years with the company, the person who trained me left for a more lucrative position at another organization and I was certain that the job would be mine. Instead, they hired someone from outside whom I had to train. I was in my early twenties and jobs were plentiful and easy to secure. Being passed over for a promotion despite my dedication left me disillusioned, prompting me to seek new opportunities. A few months later, still upset that I had been overlooked, I submitted my resignation.

The Black Power Revolution of April 1970 had just pried opened the doors of banks, insurance companies, and other financial institutions, allowing access to more people of colour. Prior to this upheaval, these businesses were traditionally the exclusive preserve of local whites, Portuguese, Syrians, and Chinese. Despite the predominance of Africans and Indians in the population, finding a Black or East Indian person in any of these institutions before then, was like finding the proverbial needle in a haystack. A mere two weeks after resigning from the company, I was offered a job with the Bank of Nova Scotia. In the eyes of the public, working in the banking industry held a certain cachet. I was hired as a Teller, and for the next twelve months, I functioned effectively in that capacity. The dress code consisted of long sleeve shirts and ties was strictly enforced. Around this time, the advocates of Black empowerment were encouraging the masses to shake off the shackles of colonialism. Since we were living in a tropical country, there was much talk about adopting a dress code that was conducive to the weather. This made sense to me, so when serving customers, I would often loosen the noose around my neck. Although I had been spoken to about my attire on several occasions, I deliberately disregarded the warnings. My defiance of the dress code led to my dismissal for "...failing to adhere to proper banking attire." While I didn't miss the job, I missed the perks, which included medical, dental, and subsidized lunches at local restaurants. For just two dollars a day, staff would purchase a chit from the bank which enabled us to dine at several restaurants in the city. Errol Lau was a cozy restaurant complete with bamboo booths and soft lighting, creating a tropical atmosphere that was intimate and romantic. Almost every day, my girlfriend and I would have lunch at this restaurant. We dined on lamb chops, beef, fish, and chicken dishes, as well as salads and desserts. Our favourite dessert was The Alamo - a slice of cake with a scoop of ice cream on top. The food was never disappointing, and although Trinidadians are not generally known for exemplary customer service, the service at this restaurant was remarkable.

As I navigated the challenges of the workforce, I realized the limitations of a high school education in securing advancement. Seeking to bridge this gap, I enrolled in evening classes at the University of the West Indies, determined to carve out a path to success despite the obstacles. Undeterred, I continued my journey in the banking sector, finding a new role at the Worker's Bank of Trinidad and Tobago. It was here that I witnessed the power of collective action, as dockworkers founded the institution and pioneered 24-hour banking on the island. The Automatic Teller Machine (ATM) was called "Mary Ann" because it was accessible all day and all night. The name referenced a folk song about a woman named Mary Ann who spent all day and all-night sifting sand on the seashore. To this day I still don't understand her rationale for doing so.

Except for a handful of troublemakers, the customers were generally pleasant, patient and understanding for the most part. At the end of each month, the dockworkers salaries were deposited, and they would descend on the bank in droves. Every customer had a bank book which had to be manually updated with information gathered from large stacks of computer printouts. Due to the manual nature of the exercise, everyday hundreds of customers would be waiting in line for extended periods to transact business. The situation became exceedingly worse at month's end when salaries were due. To add insult to injury, the air conditioning unit would routinely break down, causing the temperature inside the bank to skyrocket. On several occasions people had fainted while waiting to transact business and we were literally sweating while serving customers. To reduce waiting time, I would routinely serve as many as five customers at once. I would take their books into the vault, flip through hundreds of pages in the database, update their books, verify that salaries were deposited, and the funds requested were available. Once, in my haste to serve customers in a timely manner, I mistakenly returned the wrong book to a notoriously cantankerous customer who quickly seized the opportunity to entertain the crowd at my expense.

"Whahappen"? He shouted,

"You's ah clong or what?"

"You cah read?

Already simmering in a foul mood due to the pace of work and the oppressive heat, his comment was the final straw. Unfortunately for him, he had chosen the wrong person at the wrong time. In frustration, I hurled his passbook across the lobby. His attempt at humor backfired, causing the bank to erupt in laughter. Humiliated, he threatened to confront me after work. He vowed to meet me behind the building, goaded on by the crowd's laughter and encouragement. From behind the counter, I vocally welcomed the challenge, posturing as if eager for the encounter. However, much to my relief, when the workday ended, he was nowhere to be found. Expecting repercussions for my unprofessional outburst, I was surprised to face no consequences. However, subsequent encounters with him were notably more respectful.

Reflecting on the incident, I regretted reacting out of frustration. However, as a society, we don't often adhere to the notion that "the customer is always right." While this benefits employers, it did little to soothe the bruised ego of a young man still navigating his way into adulthood.

As the end of the month rolled around once more, the malfunctioning air conditioner exacerbated the already hectic atmosphere in the bank, posing concerns about health and safety. It was also Friday but, the manager insisted we stay behind to reconcile an account. We proposed coming in on Saturday, but he remained adamant. Despite his insistence, I refused to work but reiterated my willingness to return the following day. He interpreted my resistance as an act of insubordination and an affront to his authority. Refusing to comply, I returned the next day, only to discover I was no longer employed.

Though I had spent two years at the bank, I wasn't fazed by my dismissal. Banking no longer held my interest, and I was eager for a change. Despite the significant sums of money, I handled every day as a Teller, my salary often fell short of the next pay period.

Despite the trials and tribulations, each experience taught me valuable lessons about resilience, adaptability, and the importance of continuous learning in the ever-evolving world of work.

Recognizing the need for change and inspired by the apparent success of certain representatives, I ventured into the business of insurance. This career shift marked a turning point in my life, granting me autonomy and unlimited earning potential. It was a profession I embraced wholeheartedly for the following seven years before eventually immigrating to Canada.

As a Broker, I focused primarily on selling Life and Disability Insurance policies. My success in this area, qualified me for prestigious sales conventions in Mexico, Brazil, Barbados, and Jamaica. Just one of a handful of brokers hailing from the Caribbean and the Americas. As I luxuriated in the opulence of five-star hotels nestled in these exotic havens, I often had to pinch myself to confirm that this surreal experience was indeed my reality. The notion of having every whim catered to was nothing short of dreamlike. Despite the glamour, my humble beginnings served as a constant reminder that I could just as easily have been the one providing service rather than receiving it. This awareness kept me grounded, particularly as I bore witness to the stark poverty that coexisted amidst our tourist luxuries.

My first encounter with abject poverty occurred in Acapulco, Mexico, during an insurance convention in 1986. Amidst the backdrop of excessive wealth, I witnessed a distressing scene: a baby wearing only a soiled diaper, scrambling on the pavement to retrieve a fallen cookie. Nearby, a destitute elderly woman, possibly the child's grandmother, sat against a wall with outstretched hands. Despite the throngs of tourists bustling about, the old woman and the child seemed invisible, ignored by passersby who actively avoided making eye contact. This poignant moment struck me deeply, especially as my own daughter was around the same age. Having grown up poor myself, this level of destitution was jarring. The memory of that scene has lingered with me over the years, casting a shadow over subsequent vacations. While I've encountered poverty in various countries since then, my first encounter in Mexico remains the most vivid memory from that sales convention.

Shortly after entering the industry, I was able to establish a comfortable lifestyle, though one that could have been significantly enhanced had I chosen to remain on the island. Yet, the limitations of island life, coupled with societal divisions based on race and social status, felt stifling. These divisions fostered false notions of superiority and hindered both individuals and the nation from reaching their full potential. It was one of many factors that influenced my decision to relocate to Canada.

While I may have enjoyed a limited level of success during my time in Trinidad, success, I realized, is a relative concept. In a society of over thirty million, if you're not part of the 1%, you're simply another face in the crowd. Like the Cascadura, I sought a more accommodating environment and found myself swimming in a much larger pond. In this new setting, I discovered anonymity, allowing me to reassess my definition of success. It's no longer about material accumulation, but rather about enriching experiences and cultivating meaningful relationships with a diverse array of friends and family. The true treasure I seek now is knowledge. In pursuit of this, I continually invest in expanding my mind, knowing that it's the key to manifesting what truly matters to me.

Family Relations

The proximity of my sister's home to my office in Trinidad offered me a delightful perk. Chalice, the eldest among us siblings, exuded a kindness and generosity unparalleled. Raised on her culinary creations, I found solace in the comforting aroma of her dishes, each bite invoking a cascade of cherished childhood memories. Whether famished or not, I couldn't resist dropping by to savor her daily concoctions. Her trusty black cast iron pot, a cherished family heirloom, seemed to possess mystical powers, transforming any meal into a culinary masterpiece - be it curry beef, stewed chicken, callaloo, or paleau.

Despite numerous suitors vying for her hand, Chalice remained steadfast, prioritizing her commitment to her younger siblings over personal aspirations. With our biological mother's passing, she seamlessly transitioned into the role of the De Gale family's matriarch, presiding over an ever-growing clan. Though she never wed, her daughter Clytemnestra brought immeasurable joy into her life. Clytemnestra was the wife of Agamemnon, the King of Mycenae in Greek mythology. She lived a life of intrigue before being slain by Achilles. Despite its mythical prominence, the name never took root in the family. Instead, she came to be known as Kim. Her father was a Trinidadian of Chinese descent whose family owned a wholesale store, supplying dried goods to local retail businesses. The untimely death of his father derailed his dream of becoming a lawyer, causing him to quit school to help his mother in the business. Leonard was a personable man with a wry sense of humour. While Chalice was the love of his life, his daughter could aptly be described as the apple of his eyes. On her first day of kindergarten, Leonard died from a perforated ulcer that had been the bane of his existence for several years.

My mother, Edna Ruby De Gale, was born on the picturesque island of Grenada. She bore the name of one of the most affluent families on the island with business interest that includes shipping, supermarkets, and real estate, among others. One of the luminaries of the family was Sir Leo De Gale who served as the island's Governor-General from February 7, 1974, to September 30, 1978. While she did not share in the economic prosperity nor prestige of the more affluent side of the family, my mother possessed riches of her own. There is an adage that says, "A man's wealth are his children." She must have taken this to heart, as evidenced by the eight children that she bore. A woman of mixed heritage, she had Indian, African, and European blood flowing through her veins. This blood mixing was not indicative of her ancestors' loose moral fibre, but rather, the by-product of slavery, indentureship and colonization. History is replete with instances where oppressors forcefully inserted their DNA into subjugated women whose consent was deemed unnecessary, a testament to the complex historical tapestry woven through generations of colonization and oppression. During the three hundred plus years of slavery, plantation owners would give their last names to enslaved people and indentured servants.

They were considered chattel, private property no different from cows, goats, or sheep.

Raised in a community predominantly of African descent, our upbringing was intertwined with the cultural tapestry of our neighbors, including the vibrant traditions of the East Indian families. Yet, amidst this diversity, tensions simmered, exemplified by the strained relationship between my mother and our East Indian neighbor, a delicate dance between camaraderie and conflict.

I never knew the man who sowed the seeds that produced me and some of my siblings. Soon after the planting season was over, he abandoned the garden and immigrated to England where he cultivated another garden that produced fruit of a fairer variety. I was raised by my stepfather David Sam, an immigrant from the tiny Caribbean Island of St Vincent. He was the only father figure that I have ever known. We called him Daddy David, but to avoid saying "Daddy David" explicitly, we compressed the two names into one, so it sounded more like "Daa-vid." Daavid was a man of African descent and based on his physical appearance, it can safely be assumed that no DNA from any other race had ever infiltrated his bloodline. Although he had no formal education beyond primary school, he was acutely aware of domestic and international events, particularly those of a racial and political nature. He was familiar with the teachings of Marcus Garvey and kept abreast of the civil rights struggle that was taking place in America in the 1960's. That was how he developed race consciousness which he tried to instil in us. In their ongoing efforts to undermine Africans and Africa's contribution to the development of civilization, Daavid encouraged us to embrace our African heritage. His wisdom, though lacking formal education, resonated deeply, shaping our worldview, and instilling a sense of resilience against societal barriers. His mantra, "If a cat was born in an oven, that does not make it bread," echoed a fundamental truth – whatever our circumstances, our origins remain unchanged.

As a child, I vaguely remember meeting his brother and sister, but they did not come around often enough to develop a family relationship. When Daavid met my mother, she was already the mother of four children. They moved in together, and within eight short years, four more children were born of their union, separated by intervals of two years. We were evenly split in terms of gender, with me landing somewhere in the middle.

Under Daavid's guidance, we learned the power of optimism, banishing the word "can't" from our lexicon and embracing the notion that belief and determination pave the path to success. His disciplinary approach, though firm, instilled in us a sense of accountability and unity, bridging the divide between biological and stepsiblings.

My mother's expertise extended beyond conventional medicine, delving into the realm of herbal remedies and spiritual protection. From bush baths to purging rituals, she spared no effort in safeguarding us from evil forces, her knowledge passed down through generations, a testament to the resilience ingrained in our cultural heritage. Although she had no formal education, my mother had an encyclopaedic knowledge of "bush medicine" and its usefulness for treating a variety of illnesses. Whenever we complained of an ailment, she would concoct a combination of herbs for us to drink and in no time, we'll be on our feet again. For fever, coughs, or colds, she would brew teas from the extracts of Fever Grass, Cutlet Bush, Christmas Bush, and Man Bitter Man among others. When my sisters complained of menstrual cramps, a hot cup of St John's bush tea was all that was needed. One cup of that beet red concoction and menstrual pains would be gone. To ensure that our skin was neither blemished nor crusty, she would grease us down with coconut oil which she made from scratch. The hard jelly would be grated and boiled until nothing was left but the oil, containing no preservatives. With every application of this homemade moisturizer, we would shine like pennies that were recently minted.

Her knowledge also extended into the realm of the supernatural, and she did everything within her power to protect us. To ward off evil spirits and shield us from jealous neighbours that might want to harm us, she would gather leaves from various plants and subject us to weekly bush baths. To these baths, she added Rose Water, Katanga Water, Florida Water, and other liquids. Whether or not these baths had the desired effect, I cannot say. One thing is certain however, we smelled to high heavens. The baths were refreshing, but the strong smell of the liquids caused us a great deal of embarrassment and discomfort. If the bush baths did serve the purpose for which they were intended, it must have been because of the overpowering smell of the liquids that she added to the water.

To rid our blood of impurities, every Saturday mornings we were subjected to a purge consisting of castor oil, senna pods, Epsom salts, and half of an orange. The revolting taste of castor oil would linger in our throats for the entire day, every burp reminding us of its presence. Resistant to ingesting this unpleasant concoction, we would kick and scream and had to physically restrain each other. Although we all laughed throughout the process, the situation ceased to be funny when each of us were on the receiving end. After the medicine was ingested, the entire day would be spent in the washroom spewing waste. It is difficult to confirm whether this Saturday morning purging routine was effective. What is certain however, is that throughout our teenage years, none of us ever suffered from eczema, acne, or other skin-related diseases. Many of the plants my mother used for medicine grew wild throughout the community. Today, they are labelled "organic" and sold at exorbitant prices in high end supermarkets and health food stores across the globe.

In retrospect, our upbringing was a testament to the resilience of familial bonds and the enduring legacy of cultural traditions passed down through generations. Despite the challenges we faced, we emerged stronger, united by a shared history and a steadfast belief in ourselves, as children of the African diaspora.

The Reunion

After almost a year apart, my children finally arrived in the spring of 1990, accompanied by my in-laws. It was a moment of relief and joy as they landed in Canada, fast asleep from the long journey. Wrapping them snugly in warm blankets, I placed them in the car for the ride home. The chill in the air was nothing compared to what I had experienced when I first arrived, but my father-in-law, accustomed to the constant warmth of Trinidad, found it jarring.

" Allyuh hiding from de police or what?" he quipped sarcastically, unable to fathom why anyone would leave a tropical paradise for the cold of Winnipeg.

For him, anything below 25 degrees was considered inclement weather.

The drive passed in a blur as they slept. Arriving home, I nestled them between the warm blankets of Aladdin and 101 Dalmatians, their favourite Disney characters. Their improved language skills since we last met filled me with anticipation for the conversations we would share. Despite the constant stream of postcards, phone calls, and letters throughout the year, I couldn't shake the worry that they might have forgotten me. The relief of being reunited was tempered by the knowledge that recent changes immigration policies might prolong such separations indefinitely, a reality that I find difficult to fathom.

With the arrival of morning, I stood by their bed side watching them fast asleep and realizing how much they had grown in the past year. Then my daughter stirred, her eyes meeting mine with recognition.

"Daddy," she cried out, with her arms outstretched reaching for me.

In that moment, an overwhelming surge of emotion enveloped me as I lifted her out of bed and held her tightly against my heart. Despite the time and distance apart, she had not forgotten. As I showered her with kisses, my son awoke, startled by the unfamiliar presence. It took reassurance from his mother before he allowed me to embrace him. In that very moment, I was the happiest man alive.

In the days that followed, we embraced the novelty of snow, venturing to a nearby park where they experienced tobogganing for the first time. Their laughter echoed as we descended the slope, but a close call with a tree prematurely halted our fun. I was at the top of the hill when the toboggan suddenly veered off course and headed towards a tree. My heart leaped as I stood watching helplessly at what was sure to be a life-threatening accident. Inches before it would have collided with the tree, the toboggan came to a complete stop. Oblivious to what they had narrowly escaped, they wanted to do it again, but after that near collision, I had lost my nerve. I waited too long to be with them and did not want to be responsible for causing them pain. Despite their protests, we returned home, warming ourselves with hot chocolate and shared laughter.

With summer's arrival, we attended several festivals in the city, experiencing culture from across the globe. On the banks of the Red and Assiniboine rivers, people held picnics and visited the farmers market to sample an array of mouth-watering foods for which the Forks is well known. The Forks, an historic place where Aboriginal people had been meeting for thousands of years to exchange goods and services, centuries before the arrival of Europeans. Later, it became a major hub for European fur traders, Métis buffalo hunters, Scottish settlers, riverboat workers, and railway pioneers. Now, it was being visited by thousands of new immigrants from across the globe. Visiting the historic Forks Market, steeped in millennia of human activity, we marveled at its significance as a cultural hub. On account of its status as a cultural landscape that had borne witness to six thousand years of human activity, The Forks was designated a national historic site in 1974.

On weekends we drove to Lockport, home of the world-famous foot-long hotdog that made a crunching sound with every bite, by far the best hotdog I had ever tasted. From the bank of the river, we watched the locks accumulate and release water multiple times throughout the day. People flocked there to witness these mechanical marvels create controllable pools of water to facilitate the passage of river traffic.

Each moment together was precious, a testament to the enduring bond of family and the joy of reunification.

Toronto Bound

Despite the modern and multicultural atmosphere of Winnipeg, I couldn't get over the feeling of isolation, especially during the long winter months that made me homesick. My desire to attend events in Toronto, particularly those featuring Caribbean artists exacerbated this longing but the financial constraints of traveling from Manitoba to Ontario was insurmountable.

While I had grown to appreciate Winnipeg in the short time I lived there, my spouse wasn't as enamored. Within a year of arriving, she decided to pave the way for our family's migration to Toronto. Her absence allowed me to strengthen my bond with our children, making our departure from Winnipeg bittersweet.

A few months later, I loaded our belongings and embarked on a drive to Toronto, a journey spanning twenty-seven hours. It was early in the fall, and after eight hours on the road, darkness had descended upon us. Rather than continue, I rented a motel where we spent the night in Thunder Bay. Bright and early the following morning, we were on the road again. The kids were enjoying the ride, listening to nursery rhymes, playing, and falling asleep at varying intervals. After another eight hours had passed, I asked if they wanted to stop and sleep in another motel, but they insisted that I continue. Since leaving Winnipeg, I had consumed more coffee than I ever did in my entire life. Wide awake, I could feel my body vibrating. In that state of hyper alertness, I drove for nineteen consecutive hours, stopping only to eat and to use washrooms.

Fueled by copious amounts of coffee, I pressed on until we finally arrived in Toronto, trembling from sleep deprivation and physical exhaustion.

Soon after arriving in Toronto, we settled into life at York University, joining a community of couples with young children. Despite the challenges of student life, we found support among our peers, and our children thrived on campus, sometimes joining us in lectures and forming friendships effortlessly. This was a tight knit community, and we would often assist each other with babysitting needs. The kids made friends quickly, and they would play among the trees and the lush green grass that carpeted the university campus. When no one was available to look after them, they would accompany us to lectures. To stave off boredom, they were given the responsibility of collecting assignments and distributing handouts to students. Otherwise, they remained quiet and appeared to be engaged in the lectures. Although they were the only children present at our lectures, they behaved remarkably well. No one ever complained about their presence, and both students and professors were always delighted to see them.

To alleviate the financial strain and make ends meet more comfortably, I sought employment at a youth shelter. During the interview, the director asked what I did for recreation.

"I take care of my children," I replied.

Unimpressed with my initial response, she rephrased the question expecting a more substantial answer. My response however was the same, except that this time I painted a vivid picture of the relationship I have with my children. I told her that caring for them was not a stressful endeavour. If anything, it was therapeutic and a responsibility which I took seriously and absolutely embraced. I revealed that often after school and on Professional Development (PD) days, we would go in search of adventure. By way of example, I told her a story of taking them to an area in the park where a massive tree had fallen across a ravine. The tree created a bridge that enabled us to cross from one side to the other without getting our feet wet. It was approximately three feet wide and perhaps 20-30 feet long. As we made our way across this tree bridge, we imagined alligators chomping at our feet, and they would howl with laughter. On reaching the other side, we would encounter imaginary lions and tigers and bears, defeating them in hand-to-hand combat. At the end of every encounter, we went in search of new adventures. Their imaginations would be on fire, and their joy was beyond containment. They begged for more until we were all too exhausted to continue. Then I would take them home, bathe them, feed them, and read them stories until they fell asleep. These playdates were a barrel of fun for them, but for me, it was also therapeutic. More importantly, it created an unbreakable bond that grew stronger with each passing day. Engaging with my children brought us a level of happiness, unsurpassed by any other recreational activity. Raising my children was not work, but emotional therapy that came with my responsibility as a parent. Sharing anecdotes of our adventures together, I conveyed the joy and therapeutic value of our time spent exploring nature and nurturing their imaginations. My passion for parenting resonated with the director, securing me the job, and affirming the profound connection I shared with my children.

A Fractured Foundation

The decision to uproot an entire family and relocate them to a foreign country often puts a strain on even the strongest of bonds, irrespective of race, religion, or financial status. Through my encounters with immigrant families of diverse backgrounds in Canada, I've witnessed the disintegration of relationships, often sparked by financial struggles but further exacerbated by various other factors. Exposure to a new cultural perspective can ignite desires for independence and empowerment, especially among women who break free from oppressive norms. I've seen previously submissive women from cultures that have historically silenced them, blossom into confident individuals, many turning their backs on abusive relationships with the support of social service organizations.

My own marriage, though, was no exception to this trend. We were juggling academic pursuits while grappling with financial instability. With one of us holding a full-time day job and the other working nights at a youth shelter, we managed childcare between us. It was only after a particularly heated argument, that we mutually agreed to go our separate ways. However, I demanded unfettered access to my children. They meant the world to me, and I would fight tooth and nail, if necessary, to have them by my side. Furthermore, the thought of legal interference dictating my parental rights evoked images of historical injustices. Whenever I imagined myself standing before a judge to settle the issue of custody, I had visions of slavery where children were routinely taken from their parents and sold without concern for the emotional damage being inflicted. So, to avoid needless unpleasantness, we compromised for the sake of the children. Much too often, in divorce cases, courts would routinely give custody to the mother while dad is relegated to providing financial support and often granting restricted access to the children. This is based on the erroneous assumption that the mother is the more competent caregiver or that the father is reluctant to accept his responsibility. This leaves many loving and capable fathers looking like scoundrels. Since neither of us cared to be entangled in a legal battle, we settled on an arrangement that was mutually satisfactory. We understood that a bitterly contested divorce would certainly benefit lawyers but have a negative impact on the children's emotional well-being. As parents, we saw value and wisdom in compromise. She had no reason to doubt the love that I had for my children, and she knew that that love was reciprocated. Rather than engage in a bitter legal battle, we prioritized our children's emotional well-being and settled on an arrangement where they lived with her while I assumed caregiving duties during her work hours. With this agreement in place, I moved to another apartment on the campus, and despite our physical separation, life continued with minimal disruption.

Every weekday morning, shortly before she would leave for work, I would go to her apartment, prepare breakfast for the kids, dress them, and braid my daughter's hair. She had a full head of thick curly black hair that had to be combed every morning. Since I sported an Afro hairstyle in the 1970s and often braided it myself, I proved equal to the task. After school, I would help them with their homework, and they would have dinner at my apartment before returning home. This arrangement shielded the kids from the bitterness that often occurs when the family unit is dismantled. Although we have never reconciled, we continued to support each other which proved tremendously beneficial to the children.

Fathers caring for their children at home while their spouses work had long been a topic of intense debate in various quarters. I recall participating in a panel discussion on campus about stay-at-home dads and was proud to represent. Being available for my children meant that they never had to attend day-care which was prohibitively expensive. Unlike many children, my kids always came home to my love and a hot meal. They never had to be dragged out of bed on cold winter mornings to attend day-care, where children cried incessantly for their parents. My heart bled for the youngest ones who were subjected to this daily trauma. It is a heart-wrenching experience to witness a mother trying to untangle herself from her inconsolable child. The last thing she hears as she hurries to get to work on time, is the sound of her child screaming uncontrollably. That must be the most stressful way for anyone to start their day. Working the night shift, allowed me and my children to be free from that trauma. The extent to which I was involved in the lives of my children should not be viewed as an anomaly. As parents, we both had a responsibility to shield them from the fallout of our fractured relationship.

Being actively involved in my children's lives led me to create a small garden in my apartment complete with rocks, a pond, a night light and lush vegetation. The garden was designed to accommodate Sammy and Mortimer, two turtles that I had acquired. Mortimer was a dirty-looking turtle that I inherited from a neighbour who had graduated and had given up her residence on the campus. Sammy, on the other hand, was a little, green turtle about three inches long and cute as a button. The kids loved to watch Sammy swim around then climb on the rocks to dry himself in the rays of sun that streamed through the window in the early morning. When hungry, he would munch on a banana or watermelon before sliding in again for another swim. Witnessing his daily routine always fascinated them.

On what turned out to be an ill-fated day, I was cleaning the pond thinking that Sammy was hiding under a leaf in the garden. While rigorously churning the water to remove the filth that had accumulated at the bottom, Sammy suddenly floated to the surface. In a frantic attempt to save his life, I quickly laid him on his back and started CPR. Despite the numerous compressions that I had performed on his little chest, he failed to respond. Refusing to accept defeat, I continued with several more compressions, but he failed to stir, showing no sign of life. Although I knew it instinctively, after all my efforts at applying CPR, I eventually conceded that Sammy was dead. Breaking this news to my children was going to be extremely difficult, and because we all loved Sammy, I knew that they would be devastated. Picking them up after school that afternoon, they were looking forward to playing with the turtles. On the drive home, I tried to break the news to them on numerous occasions but found it more difficult than I had imagined. Finally, I summoned the courage and told them about the unfortunate accident. They looked at each other in disbelief as tears filled their eyes. To appease them, I promised to purchase another turtle, but they would accept no substitute. Nevertheless, I was determined to get a replacement. On the weekend, we paid a visit to the pet store. It was then that we found out that turtles like Sammy were on the endangered species list and were no longer sold as pets. Returning home, I immediately dismantled the garden, and gave Mortimer to a friend for her children to enjoy. That period of pet ownership being over, we moved on to other experiences, but we never held a turtle nor any other animal in captivity again. Knowing of the sad song that the caged bird sings, we agreed that birds and other animals are better off in their natural habitat.

As the years passed, moments like staying up late to watch movies with my daughter further strengthened our bond, enriching our lives with simple pleasures. Like the night Gabrielle and I stayed up until 2 a.m. watching the movie "Aliens." Despite the terrifying scenes, she showed no sign of fear, so we huddled tightly and enjoyed the movie from beginning to end. While working the night shift and managing household duties, I embraced my role as a parent wholeheartedly, debunking stereotypes about gender roles in childcare.

Spending time with my children was never a burden but a joy, as I endeavored to nurture their potential with love, education, and a strong sense of racial and cultural identity. Despite the challenges we faced, I remained committed to maximizing their potential, ensuring they flourish in a world that can be cruel to people of African descend.

The World's Smallest Bookstore

Words possess immense power, whether wielded with malice or intended to bring about change. During a search for a present for my daughter's birthday, I encountered a pivotal moment in a Toronto bookstore. My belief in the importance of positive representation in children's media was reinforced years earlier when I encountered a haunting image on the cover of Time Magazine—a dishevelled looking, traumatized African child, clutching tenaciously to her blonde, blue eyed doll amidst the rubble of her community in apartheid-era South Africa. Although that picture was taken several years earlier, the image still haunts me. I thought about the impact that such a powerful, negative image would have on black children. How it serves to undermine their self-esteem and what it says about the value of Black lives. Also, what it says to the world about those who would perpetrate such crimes against humanity based on race. A few years ago, I read about a study where black children chose white dolls over black ones because they felt that the white dolls were more beautiful. Since the images that Black children see of themselves are often negative and less than inspiring, that response is perfectly understandable. This image disturbed me greatly and served to underscore the significance of empowering children with affirming images reflecting their identity.

Determined to find books celebrating diversity for my daughter's seventh birthday, I scoured Toronto's malls. Disheartened by the lack of representation in mainstream bookstores, I found solace in two titles reluctantly retrieved from the depths of a store's inventory. The first was "Tar Beach," by Faith Ringold, an illustrated children's book and 1992 Caldecott Honour Book. The other was "Harriet Tubman and the Underground Railroad," a chapter book that was appropriate for her age. That was the full extent of his multi-cultural collection. The encounter took a sour turn when the sales representative declared,

"Black people don't read, so we don't usually carry such books", revealing a deeply ingrained bias.

Refusing to believe what I had just heard; my jaw must have dropped. He may not have had racist or malicious intentions, for as far as he was concerned, he was simply stating a universal fact. I thought my head would explode as I attempted to conceal my anger. Yet, I felt obliged to set the record straight. With a deliberately calculated level of eloquence, I proceeded to school him.

"I couldn't help but notice that other than Caucasians, you have no books depicting children from any other visible minority groups, are we to assume that they too don't read?" I asked sarcastically. Suddenly, he realized that he had put his foot in his mouth, and immediately attempted to apologize.

"I didn't mean it like that," he stated. "I was just ah, um…" he began to stutter.

As he struggled to mount a pathetic apology, I made him aware that 95% of the population of my country are people of colour and the literacy rate then was above 94%; ensuring to point out that this rate was significantly higher than the literacy rate in Canada's at that time. I spoke about the contributions that Africans had made to human civilization long before the shadows of Europeans had darkened the shores of Africa. I mentioned the library of Alexandra and the University of Timbuktu, where students from across the globe came to acquire knowledge. I spoke of Africa's stolen legacy and the origin of civilization. When my diatribe eventually concluded, he had received the full length of my tongue. Having no other practical option, I purchased the books and left him standing at the cash register, still attempting to apologize for his ignorance.

On my way home, I tried to dismiss his comment but the sound of his voice and the words that he had spoken pounded in my head like a migraine headache.

"Is this mindset prevalent throughout the society?" I wondered.

Even after weeks had passed, I couldn't dismiss his remark, it kept returning like a recurring dream. If his perception of Black people was a commonly held belief, then we must act decisively to address this very troubling issue, I concluded. With a full understanding of what had been said and considering the implications, I refused to relent. Finally, to fill the void in multicultural literature, I vowed to open a bookstore. Despite never having owned or operated any kind of business, my goal was to embark on a journey to challenge the stereotype. At the time of this encounter, I was still on campus and had given up my job at the youth shelter to focus on my final year of study. My only source of income was the Ontario Student Assistance Program (OSAP), a government loan that had to be repaid after graduation. Convinced that where there is a will, there's a way, I set a course to make the dream of opening a bookstore materialize, despite not having two pennies to rub together.

It was my final year of university, and I was spending a considerable amount of time at the library conducting research and completing assignments. Then it dawned on me that I could use my time at the library to identify companies that had published books depicting people of colour. I figured that if they had published one book, there may be others. For the next few weeks, I rummaged through the library identifying the names of publishers that met my criteria. To facilitate effective communication, I familiarized myself with terms that were commonly used in the industry. Next, I proceeded to write the publishers, informing them of my intention and that I needed copies of their current and back catalogues, having no idea of what to expect or if they would even respond. A few weeks later, boxes of catalogues were arriving at my apartment from every publisher that I had contacted. Due to the overwhelming response, I found myself with several boxes of catalogues to be reviewed. Over the next few weeks, I meticulously reviewed every single one, diligently attempting to identify images that were beautiful, engaging and with stories that were uplifting. It surprised me to find so many books depicting Black children and people of colour that were not available in major Toronto bookstores. Excited, I carefully cut the pages out of the catalogues and took them to a commercial printer to create high-resolution coloured copies. The result was the most vibrant and visually captivating images of black children that I had ever seen in living colour. However, this was only the beginning of a more elaborate plan. The images were to be presented in a manner that would be attractive and the best medium for achieving the desired effect were photo albums. The images were placed on one side of the plastic coverings with the book reviews occupying the other side. Soon, I had several albums filled with beautifully illustrated coloured images of book covers that looked amazing. There were folktales from around the world with varying interpretations of the same stories. Others depicted children living and playing in contemporary societies. Some contained adult titles such as The Moors in Spain, Blacks in Science Ancient and Modern, Stolen Legacy, The Miseducation of the Negro, and many more. There were books by Caribbean, African, and Asian authors. Biographies of people of colour whose contributions and accomplishments were not commonly known. Within weeks, I had compiled an impressive collection of multi-cultural literature, creating in the process, what may have aptly been described as the world's smallest portable bookstore.

With no access to disposable funds, I used the rent portion of my Ontario Student Assistance Program (OSAP) as start-up capital, reasoning that if the university decided to evict me, the process would linger in court for several months. While hoping that such drastic action will not be necessary, my best bet was to find a way to generate sales rapidly. Because the issue was too important to ignore, I felt it was a risk that had to be taken. Furthermore, I was fully committed to opening a multi-cultural bookstore and was not prepared to quit until that dream materialized.

Having no business experience, I confided in a friend on campus who was pursuing her Master of Business Administration (MBA). We joined forces and registered the business as a limited liability company. Our marketing strategy was focussed primarily on primary schools and Day Cares. However, we also catered to secondary schools, colleges, libraries, and universities. Selling directly to these institutions, guaranteed a steady and dependable source of income. My friend's job was to contact librarians, principals, teachers, and other education personnel to secure appointments. Having years of sales experience, my expertise lay in marketing; convincing educators that these books would boost their students' self-esteem, enrich their educational experience, and contribute to their overall development.

However, on my first day in the field, it quickly became clear that no sales pitch was necessary; the books covers were practically flying off the pages of the photo albums. Teachers saw the images of children that looked like the ones in their classrooms and immediately recognized the importance and value of these resources. Unable to contain their enthusiasm, they sent students to summon colleagues from other classrooms to view the collection. As educators, they understood the importance and the impact that these books would have on their students.

"Thank goodness," one declared.

"I've looked everywhere for these kinds of books. Finally, my students could see themselves reflected. You don't know what that would mean to them."

I smiled knowingly.

"I had no idea that books like these even existed." Said another.

"Thank you so much. My kids would love these books. I can't wait to read with them."

Without having to ask, they provided me with the names and contact information of colleagues at various schools and school boards. With no time to waste, I quickly established contact and the orders began to pour in faster than I had ever imagined. By the end of the first month, we had generated thousands of dollars in sales, significantly more than the initial start-up cost. The most remarkable thing was that I did not have a physical copy of any of the books. Teachers were buying based solely on the images they had seen in the photo albums and the accompanying reviews. Without hesitation, I took the orders and promised to have the books delivered as soon as they were available. At the end of each week, I placed orders with the various publishers, and soon boxes of freshly printed books were arriving at my apartment. While the images in the albums were visually captivating, the physical books themselves were even more impressive with page after page of beautifully illustrated images and empowering stories. It is an interesting fact to note that the smell of freshly printed books is as distinct as the smell of a new car. Whenever a shipment arrived, I would poke my head in the boxes to get a whiff of the new book scent. Soon, I was in possession of tons of books for which I had not yet paid a penny, neither did I have a penny to make a payment.

Fortunately, the response to our endeavor exceeded expectations. Teachers eagerly embraced the books, recognizing their potential to empower and inspire students. Orders poured in, and despite lacking physical inventory, we fulfilled promises, leveraging payment terms from publishers to sustain operations. I was able to deliver the books, get paid, pay the publishers, and place new orders. With every order, I requested extra copies and soon, I had a physical inventory that was available for immediate delivery. In addition to the albums, I took copies of books with me on appointments, resulting in a significant increase in sales.

As the enterprise gained momentum, I marveled at the transformative power of representation. Each fresh shipment of books brought the promise of enlightenment and empowerment. With persistence and ingenuity, what began as a response to a disheartening encounter blossomed into a beacon of diversity, fostering inclusivity one book at a time.

As demand surged, my physical inventory expanded in tandem, soon outgrowing my storage capacity, prompting swift action. I required a shelving solution sizable enough to accommodate the burgeoning quantity of books now in my possession. The solution materialized in the form of unused milk delivery crates, repurposed and lashed together to form a makeshift shelving unit within my apartment. This innovation not only resolved the storage crunch but also expedited accessibility to the books, slashing delivery times and reducing interest rates on invoices. By the close of that school term, our sales had soared, generating income to the tune of tens of thousands of dollars.

Word of our distinctive bookstore swiftly circulated among Ontario's schools, fueling heightened demand. Recognizing the company's vast potential, my partner advocated for her boyfriend's inclusion, sparking a substantial disagreement between us. With no resolution in sight, the business's downfall commenced as dramatically as its ascent. A few days later, my partner emptied our bank account of thousands of dollars, leaving me burdened with unpaid bills, pending orders, and the imminent collapse of the business.

Fate intervened as this crisis unfolded during summer vacation, a lull in school activity when ordered, books were due for delivery at the term's outset. To salvage the business, I devised a discreet strategy, necessitating the dissolution of the existing company and immediate registration of a new one. The new company's name closely mirrored its predecessor, a subtle change that went largely unnoticed. When schools reconvened, operations resumed seamlessly, fulfilling pending orders and receiving payments on outstanding accounts.

Following the partnership's ending, my determination to ensure the business's success redoubled. Assuming additional responsibilities, I spearheaded communication with schools and attended appointments. Through interactions with educational personnel, I familiarized myself with Ontario's school boards and affiliated institutions, as well as the landscape of book fairs and teacher conventions, invaluable avenues for expanding outreach. The first Book Fair that came to my attention was just a few weeks away. To ensure my participation, I immediately contacted the organizers, paid the registration fee, and secured a table at the event. This would be my first foray into a book fair, and I had no idea what to expect; except to say that instead of Mohammad going to the mountain, the mountain would be coming to Mohammad. Anticipating a significant turnout at the event, I ordered excess inventory, filled several boxes and milk crates with a wide variety of books, loaded them into my vehicle and was off to the fair. My display consisted of a blood red tablecloth, two book stands, and several crates of beautifully illustrated children's literature. These props enabled me to unveil the world's smallest portable bookstore the way I had envisioned it.

Amidst established publishing giants, the likes of Penguin Books, Harper Collins, Random House, McClelland, and Stewart, I felt dwarfed and outmatched as a sole proprietor lacking both financial backing and brand recognition. Their presence was a clear indication that I was out of my league and in over my head. I felt like an imposter, reminiscent of one of Aesop's fables. The tale cantered around a lion who boarded a ship dressed in sheep clothing. I feared that at any time, someone would shout.

 "There's a traitor on board, examine the horns."

That was how the imposter was exposed in the fable and I prayed that I would not suffer a similar fate. Although I contemplated withdrawing and accepted the loss of my registration fee, I choose to press forward, resigned to the challenges ahead. The event venue, a downtown Toronto hotel ballroom, presented a stark contrast: amidst a sea of familiarity, I stood as the lone vendor of color, greeted by indifference from established publishers but refusing to be intimidated. Despite my apparent lack of visibility, my vibrant display of multicultural literature stood out, underscoring my unique offering in a sea of catalogues. While my competitors relied on name recognition and catalogues to sell books, my approach was to provide attendees with immediate access to diverse literature, proving that innovation and passion can rival industry giants. In essence, it was a battle of epic proportion, reminiscent of the biblical story of Samson and Goliath.

Other than several boxes of catalogues to be handed out, the major publishers had no physical inventory on display. Their strategy was not to sell books on the spot but to have teachers order from their catalogues, a successful format that had long been tried and tested. By contrast, I had several crates and boxes of books for immediate sale, but not a single catalogue for distribution. Nonetheless, my display was eye-catching and impressive while theirs looked pale in comparison. On my racks were brilliantly illustrated children's books and the blood-red tablecloth added even more colour to my display. It was impossible for anyone not to be attracted to this unique collection of multi-cultural children's literature that also satisfied their desire for instant gratification.

I needed to capture the attention of eagerly anticipating teachers, some of whom had traveled from distant places like Montreal and Winnipeg, as well as various locales across the province, while many more from Toronto itself were present. This annual event allowed them to explore the city on the school board's expenses, a prospect they have always eagerly awaited. They luxuriated in hotels, savored the city's nightlife and cuisine, and returned to their schools enriched with new additions to their libraries. With limited resources, I diligently prepared for this event, determined to enhance, and diversify their current collection. The success or failure of my efforts hinged on the teachers soon to arrive.

The event took place in a downtown Toronto international hotel's banquet hall. As I did when I accepted the opportunity to direct a play in Winnipeg, I underestimated the significance of this event. Nonetheless, I believed that the publishers' distribution of catalogues alone, would work in my favor. At precisely 9:00 a.m., the doors swung open, and teachers flooded into the hall. Upon seeing the wide array of books available for immediate purchase, their excitement became palpable. They beckoned their colleagues, who eagerly descended upon my display. Before long, I found myself surrounded by teachers clamoring to buy books. Sales were brisk, with even the representatives from major publishing houses were intrigued by the commotion. Despite the day being long and what I considered an ample inventory for the event, by early afternoon, I had completely sold out. Within hours, thousands of dollars' worth of books had exchanged hands, with potential for more sales had I not run out of stock. For promotional purposes and to manage future orders, I retained a single copy of each book and accepted orders for future delivery. At the risk of sounding cliché, the books sold like hotcakes.

Throughout the day, teachers requested copies of my catalogue and expressed interest in visiting my non-existent bookstore. They shared information about upcoming events and invited me to their schools. Invitations to speak at teachers' conventions on the importance of multicultural literature also followed. Despite not being an expert, I meticulously researched and delivered compelling presentations. These experiences revealed previously unseen opportunities, igniting a passion to promote multiculturalism in schools. To expand my reach, I created a catalogue, the first of which was adorned with images of my own children gracing the front and back covers. Subsequent editions showcased multicultural literature and imagery of children from diverse backgrounds. With my catalogue circulating in multiple school systems, orders poured in from across the province and beyond. By the end of the school year, sales had far exceeded conservative projections and previous records.

Operating out of my apartment though successful, proved limiting, especially as teachers clamored to visit my non-existent bookstore. Recognizing the potential for growth, I secured a cozy storefront in mid-town Toronto. The space boasted white slatted walls, perfect for displaying the vibrant book covers, eliminating the need for additional painting. A custom-built semi-circular countertop in black and white enhanced the store's aesthetic appeal, while pot lights in the black speckled ceiling created a starry ambiance. Shelves positioned at various angles and ample seating invited customers to linger and explore. My office occupied the back, with excess inventory stored in the basement. A rotating selection of new titles in the bay window kept the storefront dynamic and inviting, establishing it as a haven for book lovers. Often, customers shared stories of how they couldn't resist purchasing books with funds airmarked for other purposes. One poignant encounter involved a teacher moved to tears by a children's story I read to her. I started to apologize for whatever may have offended her. Instead, she thanked me for reading so beautifully and with such compassion. She said that the story stirred up memories of her own childhood, and it was those memories that brought her to tears. She then hugged and thanked me for fostering inclusivity and for creating such a stimulating educational environment.

In my capacity as owner of a multicultural bookstore, I had the privilege of meeting some very interesting people, many of whom were authors and educators. I hosted book launching events and invited teachers, principals, librarians, and others to attend. On these occasions, authors read and signed their books and people engaged in conversation sipping wine while sampling au doves. I was making a name for myself, and teachers looked forward to seeing me at book fairs and teaching conventions. From the beginning, I supplied books to elementary schools, libraries, high schools, universities, and private educational institutions. Once budgets were approved, schools would place orders worth thousands of dollars. There was a huge demand for these books, and I was able to supply many of these institutions with what may have been their largest collection of multi-cultural literature at the time. Within the education community, my reputation was growing rapidly as schools ordered multicultural literature in large quantities. Unexpectedly, authors utilized my store for research and acknowledged my contributions in their publications. The books "Worlds of Wonder" and "Towards Freedom" stand as testaments to this collaboration, acknowledging my role in promoting multicultural literature.

Running the business was both bustling and physically demanding. Juggling roles as CEO, HR manager, and sales representative, my days began at 8:30 a.m. and often extended late into the night to meet delivery deadlines. As I packed boxes and prepared invoices, my children slept on the office floor nearby. Despite the exhausting hours, I found fulfillment in the challenge.

However, as the store gained traction and demand surged, balancing bookstore management with childcare became increasingly untenable. With no immediate family to assist, we made the tough choice to send them back to Trinidad to live with their grandparents for a year. Though heartbreaking to be separated again, we believed that the experience would enrich them. They would get to know other family members and to experience what it is like to live and attend school in the Caribbean. Since arriving in Canada, my children and I had been inseparable, and the thought of being away from them again was even more heart-wrenching the second time around. However, the circumstances made it necessary and one month later, they were heading back to the island.

It was late evening when we arrived at the airport, and the reality of being separated from us finally hit home. When it was time to board the aircraft, Stefan clung tenaciously to his mother, refusing to leave without her. Gabrielle on the other hand was looking forward to the trip. Dressed in a red and green kilt, a white top, and a French beret, she looked as cute as a button. After giving us a quick hug, she was practically skipping to the plane on her way to "a vacation." On the aircraft, they were accompanied by a friend who was visiting the island for the first time after being away for many years. At the time they had returned to the island, they were nine and ten years old and would have to register in school. On my way from the airport, I experienced the empty familiar feeling of loss when I left them in Trinidad for the first time. My reaction was also the same, I cried all the way home.

With them gone, I threw myself into expanding the business.

But despite our success, challenges loomed. Changes in government policies and the emergence of major retail competitors like Indigo Books and Chapters, coupled with the rise of online shopping, dealt heavy blows to our operation. Diversifying could have been a strategic move, but my passion lay solely in the marketing of multicultural books.

Eventually, unable to withstand the onslaught, I closed the store after seven years in operation. Yet, I cherish the experience. Though the venture didn't make me rich, it enriched my life in countless ways.

As a business owner, I experienced significant growth in almost every facet of my life. I saw the happiness in the eyes of children and heard their cries of joy whenever books were delivered to their classrooms. Seeing images of themselves reflected on the pages left them wide-eyed with a joy that was profound. The simple act of holding such beautifully illustrated books and seeing themselves on the covers and between the pages was transformative. Teachers would often invite me to observe the kids' so that I could see their reactions for myself. I would smile with satisfaction, for I had seen that joy many times before in the eyes of many children, including my own.

Over the life of the bookstore, I was able to pay my bills and create employment for several community members. When I made the decision to open a bookstore, I was unemployed, attending university and raising two black children. I saw the need, recognized the importance, and acted decisively to dispel a dangerous and destructive myth. The accumulation of wealth was never on my agenda. As an avid reader, being in an environment where books were readily available was payment itself. Those who are profit-oriented may say that because I acted emotionally, failure was inevitable, and they would be correct. Emotion is not a solid enough foundation on which to build a successful business that would withstand the test of time. However, closing the store was a personal choice. Since then, similar bookstores catering to diverse communities have emerged, but the struggle for independent booksellers continues. Despite the odds being against them, I hope they receive the support they deserve. Soon after the store ceased to operate, I heard a business strategist declare on the radio that it would cost as much as $100,000.00 to open a bookstore. The success of my operation over a period of seven years, proved that although it may cost a hefty sum to start a successful bookstore, determination and innovation can often defy expectations.

A Shocking Revelation

In the realm of Canadian education, children are nurtured to voice their thoughts freely, unafraid of negatively charged consequences. However, my children were in for a stark awakening when they relocated to Trinidad, where the educational landscape painted a vastly different picture. Here, the emphasis lay heavily on rote memorization, with students expected to commit vast quantities of information to memory and regurgitate it flawlessly, if they were to be successful during examinations. Multiplication tables from one to twelve were to be ingrained through relentless repetition, merging multiplication and division into a seamless tapestry of recall. Despite excelling in the Canadian system, my children found themselves falling short of expectations in Trinidad. Consequently, they were relegated to grades they had already mastered—a reality we reluctantly acknowledged and accepted.

What truly blindsided them was the existence of corporal punishment, a disciplinary measure unheard of in their Canadian schooling experience. The sight of classmates receiving physical chastisement from a teacher left them traumatized. Punishment, often in the form of flogging, was meted out for transgressions such as incomplete homework, speaking in class or perceived anti-social behavior, irrespective of any underlying factors. The ethos of "children should be seen and not heard" prevailed, squelching any notions of independent thought or opinion—a stark departure from their Canadian upbringing. Fearing the strap, they withdrew into themselves, only to find that even this self-imposed insulation couldn't shield them from the brutality they feared.

The strap, wielded like an extension of the teacher's arm, could strike a child's back for any infraction. My daughter recounted an incident where she and her entire class, endured a savage beating. Their regular teacher, absent, chaos ensued, disrupting the class. Despite my daughter's claim of innocence and her struggle to concentrate amidst the din, a teacher from an adjoining class barged in, unleashing a barrage of blows upon the entire class. My child, unacquainted with the sting of the strap until then, bore the brunt of this ordeal inflicted by the man they called "Sir." Visibly shaken, she recounted the incident to her grandfather, tears flowing uncontrollably and feeling unjustly violated.

Upon hearing her account, her grandfather, a respected figure within the school community, was livid. Storming into the principal's office the next morning, he vehemently prohibited any further physical punishment against his grandchildren. His resolute stance compelled the principal to assure him that such incidents would cease immediately. Despite my own outrage upon learning of the incident, my father-in-law's assurance that he had addressed the issue, enabling me to put my fears to rest. Thankfully, my children were spared further torment.

The incident dredged up memories of my own childhood ordeals with corporal punishment, where fear paralyzed my mind and stress inhibited learning. The news of my daughter being beaten brought back memories of the many times that I had been severely flogged in primary school. Whenever my teacher stood behind me with the strap in her hand, I would be paralyzed with fear, my mind would go blank, and my muscles would tense up. I knew from personal experience that stress caused by the threat of corporal punishment is not conducive to learning.

I dreaded that my children, might develop a disdain for school—a prospect that troubled me deeply as I recalled a merciless beating, I endured at the hands of a teacher for reasons still unclear, haunted me. His leather strap, rumored to be soaked in urine to inflict maximum agony. I was about nine years old when I felt the lash of this pee-soaked belt. I remember screaming in agony as the strap repeatedly landed on my back with full force. He then ordered me back to my seat, where I continued to cry softly. Devoid of compassion, he threatened to "give me something to cry for" if I didn't stop immediately. Afraid of being flogged again, I sat at my desk crying in silence, while tears mixed freely with the snot that was flowing from my nostrils. The next morning, my entire back was blistered and infected. Pockets of pus appeared where the belt had landed.

When she saw the condition of my skin, my mother was infuriated and marched with purpose to the principal's office. The thought of confronting the principal scared me half to death, so to calm my anxiety, she gave me a Bazooka bubble gum which I immediately put in my mouth. As we approached the principal's office, I stuck the gum to my stomach, intending to continue chewing it after the meeting was over. The principal listened to my mother's complaint and instructed me to remove my shirt so that he could see the blisters. By then, the gum had attached itself to my shirt, and as I made a feeble attempt to conceal it, they both watched seemingly puzzled and strangely amused. To this day, I still wonder what I could have done as a child to warrant such a severe beating. Even then, I couldn't comprehend the rationale behind such cruelty.

The experience of living on a small tropical island also spotlighted fleeting moments of camaraderie and cultural exchange my children experienced amidst the challenges. Their Canadian accents, a novelty among their peers, sparked fascination and imitation, fostering bonds with their Trinbagonian classmates. They embraced the melodic cadence of the Trinidadian accent, forging friendships and immersing themselves in the local culture. Despite the adversities, they relished the island's beauty, savored its flavors, and reveled in its unique charm.

Yet, amid these cultural exchanges, the perils of public transportation loomed large. The young, strong, and ignorant would go directly to the front of the bus line and forcefully wedge themselves through the door, trampling the less aggressive in the process. Buses also adhere to pre-determined routes, and after getting off at the nearest stop, passengers who live off the beaten path would have to trek to their destination to complete the journey. This is particularly challenging for those with small children, heavy bags, health related issues, or all the above. The chaos of bus travel, marked by aggression and unpredictability, underscored people's preference for private transportation. Both official and unofficial taxis, comprise the public transportation network, offering flexibility that buses cannot accommodate. For a fixed price, they would pick up and drop off passengers along a designated route. However, for a few dollars more they would gladly veer off the main route to further accommodate passengers. However, despite public service warnings, the wearing of seatbelts and clearly posted speed limits are interpreted as recommendations rather than the rule of law. This creates a culture of recklessness that frequently results in carnage. To maximize income, drivers would push their vehicles to full capacity, turning around quickly, only to endanger the lives of another carload of passengers. Their disregard for safety regulations and penchant for recklessness posed grave risks, contributing to the alarming toll of road accidents annually. Because the safety of passengers is the least of their concern, "Carnage on the Road" is a regular headline in the local newspapers. Death due to vehicular accidents, routinely rises above 500 victims annually, yet this vexing problem persists year after year, showing no signs of abating.

It was against this backdrop that news of my son's involvement in a taxi accident surfaced. Allegedly caused by the driver's speeding and evasive maneuvers, the incident underscored the hazards of navigating Trinidad's roads. Determined to ensure my children's safety, I resolved to return them home as soon as the school term ended. While there, I took the opportunity to transform the journey into a long-overdue reunion and vacation.

One of my first stops soon after arriving on the island was to visit Layon Hill, the area where I had spent much of my formative years. Among Belmont's many hills, this was one of the steepest, serving as a vital link connecting Belmont Circular Road to St. Francois Valley Road. For the young and physically fit, traversing the entire hill took over an hour, while the elderly and the ailing required frequent stops to complete the journey. It is quite possible that the first Africans who settled on this hill were runaway slaves. The rugged terrain would have served as a natural deterrent to anyone attempting to apprehend and return them to servitude. I am not certain if that is how the area was initially populated, but this is well within the realm of possibility. Others would have arrived after slavery was officially abolished. In the ensuing years, the hill became a base for new immigrants from Grenada, Barbados, St. Vincent and other Caribbean islands, seeking to establish a foothold on the island.

The west end of the hill was built to accommodate foot traffic, while motorized vehicles could only ascend the summit via St. Francois Valley Road. Yet, the daunting gradient didn't deter truck drivers from taking on the challenge akin to scaling Mount Everest.

From Belmont Circular Road in the west, one had to ascend dozens of steps, followed by another set before encountering a brief respite. The journey then became a continuous uphill endurance battle to the top, followed by a steep descent towards St. Francois Valley Road. My old home was situated just shy of the halfway mark. Because of the spaced-out houses, the elevation demanded considerable effort to reach. Ascending these hills, whether by foot or motorized vehicle, required endurance, nerves of steel and a vehicle with ample horsepower. Maneuvering a vehicle was a test of precision; a slight misstep could lead to a fatal plunge over the edge.

While attempting to ascend the Hill in a vehicle ill-suited for such terrain, the perilous journey nearly resulted in a tragic outcome for both myself and my companion. Hindered by insufficient horsepower and tires that had long ceased to provide adequate traction, our progress up the rain-soaked incline was hindered. Midway through the ascent, the vehicle began to slide backward, prompting a frantic struggle to regain control and prevent calamity. Miraculously, we managed to stop its perilous descent just shy of the precipice. However, despite the inherent risks, a visit to the summit of Layon Hill on a clear day promises unparalleled views of Venezuela's mainland and the expansive Caribbean Sea beyond.

This isolated community, just thirty minutes from Port of Spain, the island's capital, was predominantly inhabited by immigrants from various Caribbean islands. They lived alongside a small East Indian population, whose ancestors were brought from India as indentured servants to labour on the sugar cane plantations after slavery was abolished. The hill's elevated terrain may have initially sheltered runaway slaves seeking refuge, while later immigrants from several other Caribbean countries made it their home, shaping it into a bustling community.

At the time my family arrived on the hill, shacks of precarious construction, dotted the area. Within a short time, my mother was able to purchase the land and erected a substantial house that was still standing like a beacon on the hill. Determined to see the area one more time before returning to Canada, I made my way to the top where the full expanse of the Caribbean Sea and the entire area where I had grown up was laid before me. Suddenly, I was awash in nostalgic memories of my childhood as I beheld the familiar sights.

Childhood on Layon Hill was marked by endless summer adventures fueled by imagination. The plum tree that grew in our backyard was a retreat for storytelling; a sanctuary where we consumed plums with copious amounts of salt and pepper. Despite limited means, we embarked on imaginary journeys, exploring oceans and galaxies while lying between its gently swaying branches with the warm wind lulling us to sleep. On very rare occasions, we would be treated to Royal Castle, the tastiest chicken that was ever fried. The tantalizing aroma would cause anyone within smelling distance to salivate like Pavlov's dogs. This chicken made such an impression on our young minds that we made a pact never to share it with our children if we ever had any, locking pinkies together to seal the deal.

The neighborhood children, brimming with energy and creativity, crafted scooters from wood and repurposed bicycle parts into rollers. Days were filled with games of marbles, football, and cricket, with mishaps serving as valuable lessons. Mango foraging expeditions yielded various varieties, with Julie reigning supreme. Mangoes were savored in various forms, each more delicious than the last, embodying the essence of culinary creativity comprising chows, chutneys, jams, jellies, curry, and pepper mango, all of which were ridiculously delicious and finger-licking good.

While the bush offered a generally safe environment, its eerie ambiance dissuaded solitary exploration. Towering trees, mysterious sounds, and an unsettling atmosphere deterred most from venturing alone. One day, while my brother and I were harvesting mangoes, a man of East Indian descent, his appearance disheveled and wild, emerged from the bush wielding a machete.

"Gee meh de F#%@* bag," he demanded, his tone menacing.

In fear, I surrendered the bag, hoping for a swift departure.

"Pick up de res from de gron and put dem in de bag," he commanded, his threats looming with the glint of the blade.

Unaware that my brother was in the tree, hidden among its foliage, he continued to bark his demands. To create an opportunity to escape, I continued picking up mangoes, gradually distancing myself from the tree. When the moment was ripe, my brother leaped, and we fled in opposite directions. Reuniting later, we hastened home, relieved to have evaded potential harm. That was the last time we ventured into the bush alone, opting for companionship as a safety measure.

Our childhood fascination with cowboy movies led us to emulate the actors, despite our African descent. Unaware of the historical context and ignorant of the atrocities committed during colonization and slavery, we naively cheered as cowboys triumphed over indigenous peoples. Our education, centered on European narratives, left us uninformed about our own heritage, instilling a sense of inferiority, and perpetuating a skewed perception of history.

Casting my eyes towards Queen's Park Savannah, recollections of youthful days flooded my mind. Flying kites amidst the 1960s' jubilant celebrations, we were unwitting participants in our nation's independence festivities. Drawn into the spirited procession, we abandoned our kites, joining the revelry until nightfall. The rhythmic steelpan music and exuberant camaraderie left an indelible mark on our memories, resonating long after we surrendered to sleep.

Childhood pastimes abounded, including the craft of kite-making. Resourceful and determined, we fashioned kites from humble materials, ingeniously utilizing the spines of coconut leaves and discarded garments. Our kites were made with brightly coloured tissue paper or "kite paper," as we called it. When we could not afford kite paper, we used brown wrapping paper that we referred to as "shop paper." Although much heavier than kite paper, it served the purpose for which it was intended. A sheet of kite paper costs only pennies but raising money requires creative thinking and entrepreneurial skills. In that regard, we collected empty bottles and sold them to the local shopkeeper. The proceeds enabled us to purchase the kite paper and thread we needed to construct our flying machines. From the pliable spines of coconut branches called cocoyea, we made the "bow" and "straight piece". A mixture of flour and water produced an adhesive that we used to stick the components together. Old garments that no longer served the purpose for which they were originally intended were pressed into service. Cut into strips and stuck together end to end, these garments became the tail that stretched from six to eight feet in length. In flight, the long tails looked like meteors or mythical Chinese dragons hovering menacingly in the sky. These graceful flying machines would rise as high as the thread attached would allow. Gliding from left to right, ascending then diving down as effortlessly as a bird of prey, they performed the most impressive manoeuvres. Inserted in their tails were thin pieces of razor blades while grounded glass mixed with an adhesive was generously applied to the thread. This mixture called "mange" made the thread rough and capable of cutting, converting these beautiful flying machines into weapons of war.

From morning to night, dozens of kites would be engaged in battle, with thread rubbing against thread and tails moving gracefully across the sky. Since any physical contact could be fatal, the flyer's ability to stave off attacks determined how long his kite remained airborne. Realizing that he is under attack, the flyer will made defensive manoeuvres to evade the attacker. The coarseness of the thread would provide some resistance, but when the tail of one kite crosses over the thread of another, the kite would go sailing into oblivion. The crowd would shout "hi-yo" as the stunned flyer is left holding the limp thread in his hand, looking on in disbelief while his kite slowly disappears in the distance. The strength of the breeze would determine its final resting place. A flyer with a deep attachment to his kite would walk for several kilometres to retrieve it, often from the branches of tall trees or electric poles. If his quest to retrieve his kite was successful, he would return to seek revenge in yet another battle. These makeshift creations soared gracefully, lasting as long as skill and strategy prevailed.

Spinning tops and pitching marbles filled our days with excitement and camaraderie, while encounters with nature, like encountering snakes in mango trees or enduring coconut tree mishaps, taught us valuable lessons about our environment.

A finely made top could be purchased from a local woodworker for five cents, a significant sum for kids living on the margins of society. A common trick was to catch the top in the palm of one hand, let it spin across our shoulders and down the other arm. When that ceased to amuse us, we did battle in a game called "Jig." One top would be placed in an upright position on the ground while the other player used his to try to destroy his opponent's, rendering it incapable of spinning. Positions would alternate when one player misses the target. Many of us would be left crying over the destruction of our tops but would be back in the game as soon as we could raise the money to purchase another.

Pitching marbles was another of our favourite pastimes. In a game called "Long Dab for Bokee," the opponent would place his marble behind a rock or mound of dirt, partly obscuring its view. From as far away as six to eight feet, we would knock that marble out from behind the obstacle with the skill and precision of a sharpshooter. The player whose marble was displaced received three very painful hits or bokee on his knuckles with a marble, as the name of the game implies.

More commonly, a ring would be drawn in the dirt, and several regular-sized marbles would be placed inside the circle. The game could involve two or more players where strategy, precision, and a bit of luck were the major determinants of success. A Big Goonce or a Slug, the designated pitching marble, also called a "Tor," was used to knock the others out of the ring. The Big Goonce, an oversized marble that was four times the size of a regular one, while a "Slug" was a steel ball bearing much heavier than the "Big Goonce." These designated pitching marbles could knock several regular sized marbles out of the ring simultaneously on account of their size and weight. When a pitcher misses, positions would be alternated. In the end, whoever is left with the most marbles was declared the winner.

With no restrictions to how far we may venture, we became intimately familiar with our environment and took the opportunity to explore every inch of it. Always looking out, we learned from each other's experience.

A rotten branch had broken off from a mango tree that I had climbed, creating a hole in which a black and white snake was sleeping peacefully. On seeing the snake, I panicked and leaped from the tree landing on the ground several feet below. The incident generated a great deal of conversation, evolving into several hypothetical scenarios that got increasingly ridiculous with every telling of the story. More importantly, we learned that snakes are capable of climbing trees and were always mindful of that whenever we came across trees with broken branches.

Another time I climbed a coconut tree wearing a pair of short khaki pants that were once a part of my school uniform. I had almost reached the top when my arms and legs began to burn and shake involuntarily. Unable to maintain my grip, I slid down the tree, picking up speed on my way to the bottom. On reaching the ground, the skin on my chest and between my legs had peeled away, exposing white flesh where once the skin was dark. My friends laughed and declared that I got a white man. This was a condition where white flesh is exposed just prior to the blood oozing out. Getting a white man was a rite of passage. As painful as that experience was, it's difficult to imagine growing up in the Caribbean without sustaining such injuries.

Occasionally there were fights or rather confrontations more aptly described as scuffles. We held on to each other, fell to the ground, and rolled around until we were pulled apart. The misunderstandings that resulted in scuffles would last no longer than a day or two. We needed each other for team sports, so we held no grudges, and soon, we were playing together again as if it had never happened.

Scuffles among friends were transient, mere blips in our close-knit community, swiftly resolved without lingering grudges. Bonded by shared experiences and a collective spirit, we forged friendships that epitomized the resilience and camaraderie of our youth.

Within walking distance from our community was a labor union hall offering recreational pursuits such as table tennis and musical enjoyment from its jukebox. For a quarter, patrons could curate a playlist of five songs, seamlessly played in chronological order. During the presence of union members, the jukebox resonated with music throughout the day. Otherwise, the hall exuded a serene ambiance, interrupted solely by the rhythmic bounce of the table tennis ball and our spirited exchanges during gameplay. While union members held priority access, we generally enjoyed uninterrupted play, indulging in exhaustive matches.

On a day devoid of funds, a creative suggestion emerged among us to manipulate the jukebox by inserting a flattened soft drink cork. Remarkably, the ploy succeeded, and the jukebox churned out songs at random, without human intervention. However, our covert operation was short-lived. After several hours, a vigilant union member uncovered the subterfuge, leading to our swift expulsion and banishment from the premises. Many years would pass before I would again encounter a table tennis board.

Revisiting my childhood memories from atop the hill, forgotten events flooded back, including a poignant tale from my primary school years. Eager anticipation had built for the

Carnival bazaar, a coveted event where three classmates, objects of my youthful infatuation, beckoned. Despite a stain on my only decent shirt, I adamantly insisted on attending. Through tearful negotiations, my mother relented, pressing the stained garment into service. The bazaar unfolded in a jubilant symphony of sugary treats and infectious music. Dancing amidst the throng, stains forgotten, I reveled in the euphoria of the moment. That day I was in heaven and would have danced all day and all night. However, at exactly 6 p.m., the music abruptly stopped, and without warning, the bazaar was over.

In an instance, another reminiscence ensued, recalling a mischievous escapade with my brother to impress a girl from our school. Mounted on a rickety bicycle we had assembled from spare parts, we showcased audacious feats to garner her attention, culminating in a calamitous crash. Bruised and humiliated, we retreated, our grand gesture met with laughter rather than admiration.

Reflections turned towards Christmas in the Caribbean, a cherished time steeped in community and tradition. I thought of how Christmas in Canada is a vastly different experience for my children. After living in Canada for many years, I am yet to hear sleigh bells ring and see people dashing through the snow in one-horse open sleighs. In fact, the only ringing I hear are cash registers at the mall and people dashing into heated buildings to shield themselves from the bitter cold. My experience of Christmas in a winter wonderland was disappointing, culminating in a drain on my finances and a fraying of my nerves. If given a choice, I'll take a green Christmas any time. Having acquired a more comprehensive understanding of history and the role of Christianity in the enslavement of Africans, I've become a cynic, infused with Scrooge and possibly the DNA of the Grinch who stole Christmas. But it was not always like that. Time and the realities of life can do much to dampen the spirit of Christmas anywhere.

While growing up in the Caribbean, I had always looked forward to Christmas. It was a time of innocence, but what made it special was a sense of belonging to a community steeped in culture and tradition. We never allowed our wretchedness to hinder our imaginations. On Christmas day, neighbourhood kids came together to play "Cowboys and Indians". Those of us who Santa had forgotten, would shoot with imaginary guns using pointed fingers or pieces of sticks, complete with sound effects. We became upset when our imaginary bullets hit its intended target and the victim refused to play dead. We often threaten to leave the game but never did.

Christmas preparations began months in advance as parents stockpiled items of food and drink that we were forbidden to touch. The night before Christmas, a drum containing a pig's leg would be placed on three rocks with an iron grid separating it from the fire below. While the ham was boiling in the pot, we stoked the fire adding wood as fuel to keep the flame alive. To enhance the flavour and amplify the aroma, shadow bennie, scotch bonnet peppers, thyme, cloves, and other aromatic spices were thrown into the bubbling cauldron. The aroma made the entire community smell like an open kitchen. Throughout the neighbourhood, bread, cakes, pastels, and other mouth-watering foods were being prepared. Children fought for the privilege of licking the bowl in which the cake batter was mixed.

Predictably, my sister's godfather, who never visited throughout the year would be the first to grace our home with his presence. Bright and early Christmas morning he would arrive on his bicycle, already intoxicated. He always brought us sweets and gave each of us a penny or two and say,

"Buy something nice for yourself."

After consuming several more drinks and catching up on the events of the past year with our parents, he would leave to visit other friends and relations, wobbling precariously on his trusted bicycle as he peddled along.

Shortly thereafter, the festive sound of Parang would be heard in the distance. A mash-up of Amerindian, Spanish, Mestizo, Pardo, Cocoa Panyol, and African music. Parang is the soundtrack to the Christmas season. A band of Paranderos would go from house to house throughout the community, serenading families with cuatros and chac chacs and spreading the spirit of Christmas. Traditional food and drinks, including ham, black cake, sorrel, punch-a-crème, and ginger beer, were served. Alcoholic beverages provided the fuel that kept the spirits high, and thinly sliced pieces of ham kept the taste buds alive. While some would mix their drinks, others would chase it with a monkey's face, an indication of the drink's potency.

The Paranderos brought the spirit of Christmas to every household, injecting a spirit of joy that was palpable. Families looked forward to this annual visit and ensured that preparations were in place well in advance of the festive season. Moving from one house to another, they were spreading the spirit of Christmas. Eventually, the music would fade in the distance, leaving us with the feeling that something magical had occurred. It was as if the spirit of Christmas had descended upon a poor community, undeniably rich in culture and steeped in tradition. For that fleeting moment, the world seemed right, until the next day when the sun shone its light upon a wretched people, weighed down by the burden of living, but with spirits yet unbroken.

Descending from my musing, I navigated through the city, noting the stark transformations since my departure. Modernization had altered the landscape, yet persistent social issues lingered, underscoring the enduring struggles faced by marginalized communities. Recollections of life under British rule and subsequent independence underscored the persistent challenges of socio-economic disparity and violence, a sobering reminder of the complexities of Caribbean society.

During my formative years, numerous notorious figures traversed the streets of Port of Spain, among them the infamous Dr. Rat, whose name aptly reflected his appearance. He stood tall and lean, towering in the eyes of a child, with bloodshot eyes peering out from his narrow face and a thick bottom lip hanging low. His lean, veined arms added to his imposing presence, and his deep, commanding voice struck fear into the hearts of many. Despite being cautioned against making eye contact, my curiosity often compelled me to observe him from afar. Dr. Rat and his ilk operated outside the boundaries of conventional law, their actions either a response to societal exclusion or a means of survival. Yet, their violent exploits elevated them to legendary status as bad Johns.

Legend has it that the original Bad John emerged in the form of John Archer, a Barbadian immigrant who clandestinely journeyed to Trinidad in 1887. With 119 criminal convictions spanning his lifetime, he became a familiar figure within the legal establishment. In 1902, the Mirror Newspaper dubbed him "Bad John," a moniker that endured. Despite his frequent encounters with the justice system, Archer's audacious behavior persisted. His death in 1916 marked the beginning of a legacy associated with individuals unafraid to flout societal norms. These figures, the precursors to the steel band movement in Trinidad, instilled fear in the community, with parents cautioning their children, particularly daughters, against associating with characters that many regarded as tarnished. Affiliated with various bands, Bad Johns played integral roles in the violent clashes that marred carnival celebrations involving bands like Desperadoes, San Juan All Stars, Renegades, and Tokyo among others.

Despite attempts by the colonial powers to curb the violence through threats and legislation, carnival festivities persisted, amplified by the percussion instruments that formed "The Engine Room," the heart and soul of carnival.

In my adolescent years, I engaged in the customary activities of "pushing pan" and waving flags, experiences that offered a sense of liberation and enjoyment. Subsequently, I ventured into playing the steelpan, only to realize that I was bereft of musical talent.

During my time on the island, I embarked on a journey of nostalgia and change, reconnecting with friends, many of whom had either left for brighter horizons or had since passed away. As the week ended, bidding farewell became inevitable. During their year-long stint on the island, my children had forged deep connections within the community, feeling a profound sense of belonging. They roamed freely within defined boundaries, forming friendships that would endure beyond their departure. Their farewell drew a crowd, including an elderly neighbor who cherished their presence. Emotions ran high as they departed for Canada, yet memories of Trinidad lingered long after their return, from strolls around the Queen's Park Savannah to beach outings with loved ones. The most enduring memento? Their Trini twang intermingled with their Canadian accents, a reminder of the transformative experience that took almost a year to relinquish.

Though I relocated to Canada over three decades ago, I have maintained a vigilant watch over the social and political landscape of my homeland. My recent visit underscored notable advancements, yet I found myself troubled by persistent challenges despite the island's abundant resources. With the aspiration of influencing public sentiment to effect change, I embarked on the task of crafting numerous articles addressing various societal issues.

Among these contributions was an examination of the then Prime Minister, embroiled in a corruption scandal that threatened to exacerbate existing racial tensions and further fracture the nation. This piece, along with several others, found a platform on the "Trinicenter.com" website, as well as in national newspapers.

My commitment to shedding light on pertinent issues and fostering dialogue remains unwavering, fueled by a deep-rooted desire to contribute positively to the collective well-being of my homeland. The following are a small sample of the articles that I had diligently penned over the years.

Published Articles

"The fault, dear Brutus, is not in our stars, but in ourselves..."
--From Julius Caesar (I, ii, 140-141)

Maybe it was an oversight or even a temporary lapse in judgment that landed Mr. Panday in the penitentiary. Having once ascended the commanding heights of power, some may even argue that it was a feeling of invulnerability or the dizzying effects of power that intoxicated Mr. Panday, resulting in a lapse in judgment. Whatever the reason, the crux of the matter is that Mr. Panday is a citizen of T&T and is not above the law. Consequently, if he perpetrated the crime, he must do the time. This does not detract from Mr. Panday's tremendous contributions as a Trade Union leader and his reputation as a political pit bull. That is already enshrined in the annals of West Indian political history and will forever be attributed to him. However, to give Mr. Panday a pass because of past performance, age or status is to make a joke of justice and set a negative precedence for a nation that is in the thaws of escalating crime and unprecedented violence. This most recent development is yet another chapter in the saga of Basdeo Panday.

Mr. Panday is now the highest-ranking person in T&T politics to be incarcerated. However, he joins an elite group of megalomaniacs internationally, who breached the public trust and overestimated their vulnerability. What is even more significant is that the imprisonment of Mr. Panday happened at a time when law and order in T&T is under siege and violence and corruption have become the established norm. Relatively speaking, Mr. Panday's' sentence is short despite what his supporters may argue. Nevertheless, it sends a clear message to lawbreakers at all levels that they will pay for their crimes regardless of who they are. I hope that this is only the beginning of the war on crime. I look forward to the jailing of all those who ingratiated themselves to the public, then breach that trust by plundering the public purse. The large-scale importers of guns and drugs that rob children of their innocence and the precious gift of life must also join Mr. Panday – preferably in solitary confinement. The long hand of the law must restrain that cabal of "respectable criminals" that set the tone for the escalation of crime in the larger population. Getting rid of those rotten apples may allow good people and visionaries, to come forward and rescue the country from its downward spiral, as the nation is now experiencing capitalism at its very worst. In this country where human life is much too easily dispensed with and materialism has become the new Messiah, it is imperative that justice be swift, severe and across the board. Given the existing scenario, it will be irresponsible to allow Mr. Panday to walk Scots free. As a lawyer and a man who once ascended the pinnacle of political power, he should be a model citizen and not compromise his integrity for financial gain.

Apart from the issue which landed Mr. Panday in jail, his demise should come as no surprise to political observers. His viciousness over the years, his refusal to graciously surrender the leadership of the UNC for the greater good and a myriad of self-serving personality traits, were ominous signs of his impending destruction. As the saying goes, 'you reap what you sow." Mr. Panday himself said, "Politics has its own morality." Thankfully, the law of the land does not subscribe to that morality. As Mr. Panday made his bed, so must he lie on it. Some may say that this is destiny, but like Caesar, I too believe that "the fault, dear Brutus, is not in our stars, but in ourselves."

The following article addressed the immigration issue and the opportunities that newly arrived immigrants were getting ahead of locals.

Rumours of War
By: Michael De Gale
Date: 8/20/2008, 11:53 am

As wars, restlessness, employment, and investment opportunities make it necessary for people to move, immigration in the new global economy has become a fact of life. Because of its wealth, T&T has become a particularly attractive destination for immigrants from across the globe. Evidence suggests that most of these immigrants are doing exceptionally well, establishing businesses, and accessing supports from government and financial institutions that traditionally deny similar services to locals. As an immigrant myself, it is nice to feel welcome in your adopted home and be able to take advantage of the opportunities provided. What troubles me, however, is that native born Trinbagonians on the lowest rung of the socio/economic ladder, continue to scrape the bottom of the barrel for opportunities while living in festering ghettos, not far removed from the days of slavery and indentureship.

To quote Malcolm X, "Sitting at the table does not make you a diner, unless you eat some of what's on that plate." This poignant statement is clearly applicable to Trinbagonians living on the fringes of the society, witnessing recent immigrants enjoying a standard of living locals can only dream about and *from all indications would never attain. They are second-class citizens in the land of their birth. This scenario breeds contempt and leave the door open for those who would use ethnic and anti-immigrant scapegoating rhetoric, to sow seeds of discontent and stroke the fires of racial hatred.*

Scapegoating is a historically divisive tactic, used over the years to stir nationalist sentiment, create discord, divert attention, and make victims of the innocent often through violent means. History is replete with examples including the near extermination of Jews in Hitler's Germany and the genocide in Rwanda. From Sarajevo to Sri Lanka, Jerusalem to Djakarta, it seems that much of the world is engaged in a war pitting one group against another. A recent New York Times article claims that there are 47 countries involved in violent ethnic conflict, including 8 in Europe, 10 in the Middle East, 15 in sub-Saharan Africa, 11 in Asia, and 4 in Latin America. Considering the widening gap between rich and poor, the scourge of violence in the society, the influx of new immigrants, race baiting by the politically ambitious and a host of other triggering factors, it is only a matter of time before T&T takes its place as a nation in conflict.

In this smouldering cauldron of race, class, and immigration, it is morally reprehensible and politically irresponsible to allow a growing underclass to stew in poverty. The violence that is claiming the lives of young people in T&T daily is evidence of a restlessness, symptoms of much deeper social problems. Punitive responses to crime without addressing the root of the problem, while providing incentives to newcomers in disproportion to locals, only adds insult to injury. CEPEP and URP programs may provide short term relief to satisfy immediate needs, but they fail to provide long-term support to launch careers, instil dignity and support families. Skill training programs, self-employment initiatives, investing in communities and access to education are integral components in the struggle to liberate people from their wretchedness. It is not charity but investing in people and communities that will stave off the kind of conflict that is plaguing nations around the world. Embarking on a reactive approach to issues that promises to be potentially explosive is a fatal mistake for any administration. If the authorities are unable to control the violence that is currently taking place, it would be impossible for them to successfully put out the fires of ethnic and racial violence that seems inevitable. As the saying goes take in front. If the authorities refuse to yield to reason before long, they will yield to force.

The Seeds We Sow
By: Michael De Gale
Date: 8/1/2008, 3:58 pm

I yearn for the day when I can look at the front page of any T&T newspaper and see headlines that are not crime related. Unfortunately, I cannot hold my breath until hell freezes over or for the incumbent government to realize that there is a direct correlation between poverty and crime.

As a matter of interest, a study about the roots of crime in Canada was recently published in the Canadian press. I am certain that much of the statistical data provided would be applicable in a T&T context. The study claims that more than 70% of persons who enter the prison system are high school dropouts; 70% have unstable employment histories; four out of every five have substance abuse problems when they are convicted; and two out of three youths in the system have been diagnosed with two or more mental health issues. In Toronto specifically, the data analysis shows that the 10 poorest neighbourhoods have the highest incarceration rates, the lowest income, highest unemployment, most single parent families and lowest level of education. I am not sure if any such study was ever undertaken in T&T, but I am willing to bet that if such a study was indeed conducted, the conclusion *will be the same, but the statistics would seem pale in comparison.*

It is instructive that in Toronto with a population more than 2.5 million, 30 mostly young people have been murdered to date. This created an outcry in the city and calls for immediate action to address the cause. Whether deserving or otherwise, the deaths of these young people abruptly ended whatever potential they may have had and robbed society of whatever contributions they may have made under different living conditions. For the last few years, the Mayor and the City of Toronto, private corporations, community organizations and individuals, have banded together in search of solutions to arrest the escalation of violence in the city. Priority Neighbourhoods were identified, and steps were taken to address the problems that frequently culminate in death by violent means. Solutions included creating employment opportunities in private companies and in government ministries for youths specifically from these neighbourhoods; financial and infrastructural investments in these communities, training and mentorship programs; community policing and investing in early childhood education to mention a few. It is still a work in progress but being personally involved in some of these initiatives, I can assure you that these investments have already begun to pay dividends. The transition from perceived thug to valued citizen is an amazing phenomenon to witness.

An intellectually bankrupt administration, who fail to tally the true cost of crime in society, will erroneously continue to view punishment as the panacea to end the problem. This study and many others over the years have all concluded, that for a fraction of the cost of enforcement, investments in poor communities and in early childhood education will significantly reduce this epidemic. The benefits will be clear in economic terms, lower dropout rates, a significant reduction in crime and, a more prosperous and progressive society worthy of developed country status.

If there is a gene that makes people prone to criminal behaviour, it is inconceivable that that gene should be disproportionately embedded in the DNA of poor people. As I have often advocated and as the study suggest (not withstanding "white collar crime"), poverty is the root of criminal behaviour. The poorest areas in T&T such as John John, Laventille, Belmont and the hills of Diego Martin to mention a few, are incubators for raising criminals. Even if by some miracle the police, army and the criminals themselves manage to successfully wipe out the current batch that is menacing the society, a new crop of criminals are now sucking on the breast of poverty, as the nation's hand continue to rock the cradle. They too will soon wreak havoc on an uncaring and dispassionate society.

In 1881 Frederick Douglas the great orator, runaway slave, newspaper editor, U.S. Congressman and abolitionist unequivocally stated that, "neither we, nor any other people will ever be respected until we respect ourselves, and we will never respect ourselves until we have the means to live respectfully." In capitalist societies such as ours, education and access to opportunities are fundamental to acquiring the means to live respectfully. The scourge of violence that is holding the nation hostage as the rest of the world stare in utter disbelief represents years of neglect and marginalization; first by colonialism and now by a government who mistakenly confuse window dressings with progress. In this once hopeful and now obscenely rich society, it is shameful that violence is the one thing that now defines us. If we fail to invest in poor communities, we will continue to reap violence - the fruit that we have sown.

If Thy Right Hand Offends Thee…
By: Michael De Gale
Date: 7/4/2007, 2:12 pm

I am not a man given to violence nor am I the fanatical follower of any religion that advocate cutting off the hands of thieves. However, the more I learn about endemic corruption in T&T, massive budget overruns and the widespread breach of public trust, the more I am convinced that there is some merit to this form of punishment. Without appearing to break bread with what some may consider barbarians, I could willingly support the law which states that, if the right hand offends you, cut it off. Not to punish poor people who steal to feed hungry children in the cornucopia that is T&T. Not even as punishment for the drug or chemically addicted who are compelled to steal to feed the insatiable cravings of the monkeys on their backs. Such people are desperately in need of professional help and social intervention.

The thieves I despise most are not the ones who steal bread to abate hunger, but rather those good citizens of despicable moral fibre, who steal so that their cups could rennet over. I refer here to corrupt politicians, holders of public office, dishonest contractors, and birds of similar feather, who feels no compunction when pilfering from the public purse and does so with impunity.

This country did not become independent from Britain so that we could trade one bunch of thieves for another. This den of thieves both native born and foreign, should not be free to feather their beds from the public purse and have their crimes go unpunished.

We have been blessed with resources and a window of opportunity to build a model nation in the Caribbean. - a nation that could rise like a phoenix out of the ashes of colonialism. Instead, we are saddled with thieves and brigands of all stripes devoid of even a molecule of national pride. Those who will fill their pockets and funnel excess into foreign economies are not people but parasites and should be dealt with accordingly.

A corporate building of blue-plated glass rises above 25 stories and stands majestically on the Canadian landscape. This impressive structure casts a long shadow in the evening sun and can be seen from many miles. I've heard it said that this building was funded with money that was stolen from T&T by a politician who took refuge in Panama. Every time I pass, I wonder how many more of these buildings are dotting skylines across the globe, paid for with T&T Petro-dollars and benefiting everyone except those from whom the money was stolen. The thought makes me sick to my stomach.

It is for this group of thieves that I reserve the sword. These shameless bastards, dishonest scoundrels posing as upstanding citizens, do more to undermine the country than the criminals who grace the daily news and strikes fear in the hearts of law-abiding citizens. As notorious as the latter are, the insidious good citizens who steals from the public is a malignant cancer in the society. Chopping off the hands of these white-collar crooks, will do much to send this cancer into remission. For it is written that; if thy right hand offends thee, cut it off and indeed, I am offended.

During a discussion with a visiting delegation of English MPs, the topic of the high level of violence in our country arose. One of the British MPs seemed to downplay the severity of the issue, likening it to problems faced in Britain. His dismissive attitude seemed to resonate with one of my old friends who had ventured into the political arena and held a ministerial position. Unfortunately, he subsequently echoed similar sentiments in parliament.

Because of my knowledge of history, I expressed my deep disappointment and concern regarding his response. Violence, regardless of its prevalence elsewhere, remains a pressing issue that demands urgent attention and concerted efforts to address. Dismissing it as inconsequential not only undermines the gravity of the situation but also does a disservice to the countless individuals and communities affected by it.

As someone who has known him since our school days, I had always admired his dedication to public service and his commitment to advocating for others. However, his stance on this matter has left me deeply troubled and disillusioned. I implore him to consider the source and to reconsider his position with the seriousness and urgency it deserves. We owe it to our citizens to tackle violence head-on, rather than trivializing it or brushing it aside as a non-issue.

I trust that he would have reflected on these concerns and take appropriate action moving forward. Our country and its people deserve nothing less. The following letter to the editor, expressed my frustration.

Mr. Hinds Should be Tarred & Feathered
By: Michael De Gale
Date: 8/23/2006, 1:00 pm

Incompetent, unconscious, unconscionable, and an imbecile, Fitzgerald Hinds is an embarrassment to the PNM, his constituency, the legal profession, and Black people everywhere. I've stopped being surprised when I hear the utter nonsense that emanates from the mouth of this brother, however, I continue to be consistently embarrassed. To state in Parliament that his British counterparts assured him that T&T is as safe as London despite the unprecedented number of murders, is a clear indication that Mr. Hinds is either a buffoon or he is just plain stupid. He certainly has no sense of history for if he did, he would understand why his British counterparts will make such a statement. How does one rationalize the fact that in a population of just over 1.2 million and an area of approximately 1,864 square miles, 253 people have been murdered to date? By comparison, in Toronto with a population of more than 2.5 million, less than 50 murders have occurred over the same period. Must we always aspire to the lowest common denominator?

Mr. Hinds should know that historically, the British has had no respect nor regard for Black life. It is therefore not surprising to learn that they do not see a problem. As long a Black youth continues to kill each other they will never see a problem. God knows that they have murdered, maimed, and raped enough of us with impunity over a period of 400 years. In that context, the fact that they are not appalled by the unprecedented number of murders in T&T is very understandable, but Mr. Hinds does not have to concur.

If Mr. Hinds should repeat such nonsense in any other House of Parliament and try to sell this as a positive thing, his resignation will be immediately demanded. Such a statement shows an utter disregard for human life and a ministry, whose leadership is incapable of effectively executing its mandate to ensure the safety of citizens. Mr. Hinds is the classic example of a mis-educated Negro, who will sell his soul and his constituents to gain the approval of and rub shoulders with those who in his mind are greater than himself.

Despite his Rasta hairstyle and deep dark hue, Mr. Hinds is a good house Negro and an obedient pet. He reminds me of the children's story called The Emperor's New Clothes in which the emperor was convinced that he looked smashing in his fine attire, when in fact he was stark naked. More appropriately, I am also reminded of George Orwell's poignant novel entitled 1984 where it became increasingly difficult to distinguish pigs from people. For vocalizing this hogwash, Mr. Hinds should be tarred and feathered. There are those who I am sure would argue that Mr.

Hinds is already tarred, OK! Then he should be feathered.

Giving It All Away
By: _Michael De Gale_
Date: 1/29/2008, 1:01 pm

The caption in the business section of the Trinidad Guardian 24/01/08 read, "Petro-Canada excited over T&T gas find." The article referred to the recent discovery of between 0.6 - 1.3 trillion cubic feet of recoverable natural gas. I am not a geologist, but that strikes me as a significant amount of natural gas regardless of how it is measured. Petro-Canada is reported to have said that the local gas discovery is among the "more significant" of its international exploration successes. What's more, this find is the first of a four well program and according to company officials, "the discovery validates our exploration model and further success on the block could lead to a material development." I am not sure what the term "material development" means but I am willing to wager a bet that the mother lode is yet to be discovered.

Nonetheless, that is beside the point. What really disturbed me about the article was the so called "partnership agreement" in which the Petroleum Company of T&T, Petro Trin, owns 10% and Petro-Canada owns the remaining 90% of the entire operation. Hell! I too would be excited if I owned 90% of any resource, especially one that is as lucrative as *oil and gas and is the birth right of other people. If this is the full extent of the agreement, one does not have to be an economist to figure out that something is drastically wrong, or somebody buckled under the pressure of high stakes negotiations. This does not strike me as a partnership but more like the 30 pieces of silver it took to give it all away. Regardless of who brought what to the table, there is no "Win - Win" situation here; there are only big winners and pathetic losers. The losers are none other than the people of T&T.*

For the sake of argument, let's say this was a legitimate agreement free of any questionable conduct or reasons to raise red flags. In such a scenario, the parties that were involved in negotiating this agreement should be barred from any future negotiations and immediate steps should be taken to amend that contract. For too long MNCs have sucked the natural resources of underdeveloped countries leaving them more destitute and wretched than they found them. It is time for that predatory and parasitic behaviour to stop. The Nigerian playwright and activist, Ken Saro-Wiwa, gave his life in 1995 so that the Ogoni people in their oil rich region could have greater control of their natural resources. Our leaders should be willing to sacrifice no less.

It is never easy negotiating with multinational corporations particularly when you feel compromised.

However, that is no reason to cower and give away your resources to the lowest bidder. In Newfoundland for example, one of the poorest provinces in Canada, the Danny Williams administration in 2005 put Exxon Mobile and other oil consortiums on notice that they would aggressively negotiate for enhanced local benefits from any agreement to develop their oil and gas resources. Premier Williams stated clearly that there will be "no more giveaways". He was unequivocal about the approach he would take to resource development: "My team has received a mandate to seize control of our own destiny," he said. "The giveaways end right here and right now." As expected, business and various conservative elements raised a hue and cry, but the premier stood his ground. Despite threatening to take their exploration activities elsewhere and vociferous public rhetoric, straw polls showed 77% in favour of "leaving it in the ground." Two years later, the consortium returned to the bargaining table and struck a new agreement with the province. Once the most destitute of Canadian provinces, Newfoundland and Labrador with its oil and gas resources is now poised to be another jewel in the Canadian crown.

My question is, how long will we continue to allow foreigners and the local elite to reap the benefits of our resources while our people languish in a country ripe with inflation, corruption, injustice, murder, armed robbery, maladministration, drug-trafficking, hunger, dishonesty, and plain stupidity, to quote Saro-Wiwa himself? The people of T&T are not asking for the moon just a bigger slice of what is rightfully theirs. It is curious that the OWTU and the once powerful Labour Congress remain conspicuously silent about this atrocity.

The Catholic Church and the Underdevelopment of Africa
By: Michael De Gale
Date: 3/19/2009, 10:53 am

Considering the devastating effect that AIDS is having on the continent of Africa, it is unconscionable that Pope Benedict XVI should condemn the use of condoms to reduce the spread of HIV and AIDS. In a recent visit to the continent where 22 million people are living with the disease, Pope Benedict XVI stated that, "condoms are not the answer to the AIDS epidemic in Africa and can make the problem worse". This begs the question, "How many more of Africa's sons and daughters must suffer and die before this hood wearing demon places human life ahead of religious dogma? Indeed, contraception is not the panacea that would put an end to this scourge, but it will do much to curb the alarming rate of infection.

More than the obvious effect of illness and death is the impact that this epidemic is having on every facet of African life, particularly in the Sub-Sahara region. Education, industry, agriculture, transport, human resources and economies in general are reeling under the strain of this epidemic. According to a 2007 conservative estimate, 17 million have died and another 25 million is expected to follow. In the past year, it is estimated that more than 15 million children under 18 have been orphaned because of AIDS. Many of these emaciated children are caring for younger family members still in diapers, when they can barely care for themselves. Like the billions of dollars in bailout money we are hearing so much about these days, the number of deaths and infection from AIDS and HIV in Africa is staggering. It is increasingly evident that HIV and AIDS continue to devastate Africa much like the trade in black flesh from which Africa and her children throughout the Diaspora have not yet recovered. With the ongoing loss of such valuable human resources, it will be a long time before Africa can emerge from this crisis, if ever. It was European greed and Christianity that precipitated the underdevelopment of Africa; now religious zealousness continues the onslaught.

For hundreds of years the Catholic Church has played a leading role in softening up Africans for European exploitation. Stripped of their ancestral beliefs and convinced that they were the children of a lesser God; they embraced a European version of Christianity and worshipped an alien God much to their detriment. In 2000 it was reported that there were over 360 million Christians in Africa with Pope Benedict XVI as their supreme leader. In the capital of Cameroon, it was reported that thousands of flag-waving faithful stood shoulder-to-shoulder in red dirt fields and jammed downtown streets for a glimpse of the pontiff's motorcade. Given the history of the Catholic Church in Africa, one can only pity the poor bastards who fail to take lessons from history, whether past or contemporary.

Although the faithful may argue otherwise, African Christians were always the bastard children of a European God, Pope Benedict makes that clear in more ways than one. Evidently, God's favoured children are of a lighter hue living in the lap of luxury throughout Europe, North America and in Africa itself. They know neither pain nor hunger. In fact, suffering of any kind is alien to their nature. While the bible tells us that the meek will inherit the earth, the Catholic church will see to it that blacks are left with nothing to inherit, when it is done under developing Africa.

Dragged Up, Dotish and Dimwitted
By: Michaël De Gale
Date: 12/18/2008, 11:44 am

The words that emanate from a person's mouth says more about them than the subject itself. They give deep insight into that person's intellect, wit, personality and may even say something about how they were raised. For example, consider this alleged exchange between Lady Astor and Sir. Winston Churchill.
Lady Astor - Sir, if you were my husband, I would poison your drink.
Mr. Churchill - Madam, if you were my wife, I would drink it.
Notwithstanding his brash personality and racist tendencies, intellect, and wit oozes from Mr. Churchill's statement. Yes, it stings but it is tasteful, brilliant, and funny, requiring no further explanation to conceal his contempt for the pompous Lady.
After a long and un-substantive presentation from an opposition member, Dr. Eric Williams when finally given the floor to comment on the matter at hand is quoted as saying,
"Like the previous speaker, I too have nothing to say".
Dr. Williams' disregard for the speaker's contribution, his own arrogance and his brilliant intellect are all very evident in that simple response. He could have said that the speaker was stupid, uninformed, intellectually

challenged and should have shut up a long time ago. Alternatively, he could have shouted him down and threatened violence as they do in Parliament today. Although the good Dr. came from relatively humble beginnings, he was sharp, witty, and certainly well raised.

By contrast, consider Mr. Panday's comment on learning of Mr. Manning's surgery for kidney cancer:

"As one human being to another, I am sorry that he is ill and I wish him well but as a politician, I think he has ruined the country and the two must be kept separate."

For a seasoned politician, it is unfortunate that Mr. Panday chose to reference Mr. Manning's politics in the same breath with which he wished him well. His feeble attempt to separate the "man" from the "politician" did nothing but reveal his own viciousness and his lack of statesmanship. It clearly points to a dimwitted, vicious old man who is tactless and incapable of deep thought. Insincerity, anger and viciousness ooze from his statement and I am certain that Mr. Manning could do without Panday's well wishes.

Regardless of what he thinks of Mr. Manning as a politician, this is certainly not the time for taking cheap political shots. Mr. Panday was once the Prime Minister, but he was never a statesman. He is intellectually handicapped, deceitful, emotionally sterile and dangerously desperate. Neither time nor power *could erase the fact that he was clearly dragged up. His dislike for Mr. Manning and his thirst to return to power is common knowledge. It is not necessary for him to feign well wishes. Mr. Manning's management of the economy is controversial to say the least. There are probably many people who hate his guts and hold no good wishes for him, but to mix politics with insincerity in a time of illness is simply in bad taste. Mr. Panday could have simply responded, "my thoughts are with him" and leave the public to ponder the nature of these thoughts. On the other hand, he could have chosen to be true to his character and say, "I've just learned about his illness. Let's hope it's nothing trivial." For that he would have been respected. Instead, he chose a cowardly way in a time of crisis to take cheap shots at his arch rival. I guess they just don't make them like they once did. It used to be said that to be a police officer in T&T, one had to be young, strong and ignorant. To hold political office in T&T these days, it is enough to be dragged up, dotish and dimwitted.*

Forward Ever – Backward Never
By : Michael De Gale
Date : 11/20/2007, 12:38 pm

It took me a while to recover from the shock of the cesspool into which local politics had fallen, and to fumigate my mind from the stench that permeated political discourse in the recently concluded general election in T&T. I will not rehash the unsightly displays and personal attacks that took precedence over numerous opportunities to articulate a vision for the country, propose feasible solutions to pressing social issues and to demonstrate enlightened leadership. However, I still can't get over the petty miscreant whose battle cry was "let ME go out in a blaze of glory", when the future of the nation was at stake, nor the acrimonious remarks used by the sore losers to concede defeat. But all that is behind us now. The universe has unfolded as it should. While there is need for consultation and strategy, the job of running the country must continue without pause for a honeymoon. At the core, it must be born in mind that a government was elected to lead a nation, not only to serve those who lent their support when political barbarians were pounding at the gates. That's what democracy and leadership is about.
Today I see the smiling faces of the newly minted men and women who survived that assault and have now

ascended to political office. Thanks to the efforts of ordinary people who believe the rhetoric and elected them to articulate their needs in the esteemed house of parliament, the palace of power. You now could demonstrate that the confidence placed in you was not misplaced. I see a rejuvenated government with a five-year mandate and ample opportunity to do right and to do more. I believe we have long passed the stage where politicians would show up once every five years with a bag full of promises they never intended to keep. The sound defeat of the opposing parties is indicative of this reality - a lesson the new office holders would be well advised to learn.

Without coercion and on your own volition, you have agreed to place yourselves at the service of the people and they've given you, their support. Consequently, they expect nothing less than your full commitment and devotion to duty. This is not about you, but you will do well to remember where you came from and how you got to where you are today. For those who may have forgotten, allow me to remind you.

You are the sons and daughters of the neighbour next door, the same boys and girls who grew up in mixed communities across the country. You are not representatives of an imperialist power bent on sucking the nation's resources and its people of their right to life itself. When I see you, I understand why people throughout the Caribbean vigorously struggled against imperialism. I see Dr. Eric E. Williams, Makandal Daaga, Dr. Cheddi Jagan, Marcus Garvey and Walter Rodney, just a handful of Anglophone intellectuals among others, who believed that Caribbean people are capable and sufficiently competent to govern themselves. I am reminded of the reason why families of African and Indian descent, slaved in cane fields and performed menial task across the land. Today, I see the fruits of their labour. In essence, you are the sons and daughters of heroes yet unsung, whose individual names would never be recorded in the annals of West Indian history.

Their struggles and sacrifices have culminated in your arrival in the corridors of power; you must now do your part to take the nation forward. Do not allow yourselves to be consumed by the dizzying heights of political office and lose sight of the fact that you are there to represent the people and the nation's interest. The fact that you are now among the political class does not exonerate you from your responsibility as elected representatives of the people. Like George - the protagonist from Earl Lovelace's penetrating novel "Salt", you carry the hopes and dreams of your respective constituencies squarely on your shoulders. Fulfill those needs and when it all comes together; the whole will indeed be greater than the sum of its parts. If you came in with an ego, cast it aside. If your ambition is to enrich yourself, may the vengeance of

Moco fall upon you, for you will be desecrating the memory of all those who paid with blood, sweat and tears to pave the way for you.

As daunting a task as it is, you have a moral responsibility to leave this nation better than you found it. I am confident that you could rise to this challenge if you remain mindful of your history and cognisant of the kind of nation we want to build in the Caribbean. Greed and self-aggrandizement will not suckle at your breast if you promise yourselves to give more than you could possibly get.

Commit yourselves to building a better nation. You must do this to commemorate those who fought to free us from the chains of slavery and the oppression of colonialism. Dedicate yourselves to duty, so that Trinbagonians can enjoy the beauty and bounty of the land we affectionately call sweet T&T, and like generations before you, pave the way for those who must follow. In the eternal words of the Grenada revolution and its inspired leader, Brother Maurice Bishop, Forward Ever - Backward Never.

Good Governance Forever
By : Michael De Gale
Date: *10/12/2007, 12:55 pm*

Mr. Manning's decision to turf the party's deadweight and replace them with a seemingly talented young group free of political baggage and eager to prove themselves, was a demonstration of decisive leadership, political fortitude, and foresight. For too long, the PNM had been burdened with parasites, dinosaurs, and political opportunists, who were nothing but an Albatross around the party's neck, weak links, millstones, liabilities and losers. For this bold and courageous move Mr. Manning should be loudly applauded.

Despite the numerous criticisms levied against him, his inflated ego and his political blunders, I have always believed that Mr. Manning is a man of integrity who has the best interest of the country at heart. Surrounded by sub-standard ministers intrigued by the idea of power but lacking the intellectual acumen and commitment to shoulder the responsibilities of high office, the party's performance lagged, and a prolonged period of public disenchantment ensued. With the recent housecleaning, that period should now be over and the PNM could look forward to the coming of better days filled with fresh ideas, farsightedness and people commitment and capable of ensuring the *country's continued development. They have five years to prove themselves capable.*

During the previous UNC administration and in this party's present bid to recapture the top political prize, it is increasingly clear that the UNC is a polarizing force in the nation despite the present of their African mascot, Mr. Warner. Under the leadership of the convicted felon and mean-spirited Mr. Panday, the UNC has no hope of ever regaining political power in T&T. As the saying goes, "they spinning top in mud". Anyone with political aspirations and good intentions will be well advised to disassociate themselves from that group of Neanderthals, who lack credibility and hope to attain political power through the destructive strategy of divide and conquer - hardly a recipe for growth and economic development. This is inconsistent with the spirit of T&T where the motto is still, "Together we Aspire, Together we Achieve". A UNC victory though highly unlikely, would be nothing but a pox upon the land.

Although a neophyte in the political arena, the COP poses a credible threat to the ruling party, but the capability of its leader is questionable. With a wide ethnic support base and enjoying a degree of popular support, Mr. Dookeran's past association with the UNC should be cause for concern. Inquiring minds want to know if he can advance the interest of the nation, or would he pander to special interest and race-oriented groups. More than that, the public toying with Mr. Dookeran for leadership of the UNC was both emasculating and publicly humiliating. Mr. Dookeran allowed himself to be strung along for much too long before COP came and arrested the problem. Even then, he looked a little shaken. One must question his ability to be decisive after being turned into a pappy-show in a game of carrot and stick. All these issues raise questions about his strength as a leader, the seriousness with which others should view him and certainly his vision for the nation.

Granted the PNM has made several blunders in the past but from inception, it was always clear that this party was a unifying force with the best interest of all the people of T&T at heart. Despite being dogged by political mongrels, contemporary / historical social issues with more than its fair share of scandal, they have managed to keep this juvenile democracy on its feet, stable and growing from strength to strength. Ample evidence around the world is living proof that this is not an easy exercise. After the recent house cleaning - which I hope is certainly not complete, I believe that the infusion of new blood into the party is a good sign. Young, educated and hopefully with vision that extends beyond the narrow confines of small island politics, the future looks bright for the PNM. Unlike the political imbecile and the illiterates who boldly proclaim, "PNM till ah dead", the people of T&T

must vociferously demand, "Good Governance Forever". Given the current line up of political aspirants anxious to rule supreme in the local corridors of power, the Peoples National Movement is well placed and capable of answering this fundamental human and distinctly democratic call.

Measuring Mediocrity
By: Michael De Gale
Date: 9/14/2007, 4:38 pm

It is a sad situation when mediocrity is the highest standard to which a nation aspires. For as long as I could remember, the people of T&T have bemoaned the poor quality of service they receive from public health, police, education, transportation and virtually all government ministries. So, I thought that people would be happy to learn about the poll which shed light on the dismal performance of many government ministers. Yes! A poll was needed to identify these slackers as much as a light is required to see the sun. Nonetheless, the pole confirmed what the public had always known - government ministers are incompetent, lack vision and are incapable of fulfilling the mandates of their ministries. Despite all appearances, they are trapped in a Third World mentality. How else can one explain the sorry state of social services in T&T?

As a young high school student, I once scored 45% in a test and emerged first among equals. While I felt like a horse in a jackass race, even at that tender age I knew that my performance was abysmal and I had nothing to be proud of. Imagine my surprise then, when Minister Raphael crying crocodile tears, announced that he will not be contesting the upcoming election. Apparently, he honestly thought that he was *doing a good job even as the public is bombarded with news and disturbing images of medical atrocities in public health institutions daily that would not be acceptable anywhere else in the civilized world. Talk about delusional. What is even more disturbing are the members of his constituency who spoke out in his defense. Are Trinidadians such a narrow-minded people that they will sell the nation's health system for 30 pieces of silver? If that is the case, may God have mercy on the nation's soul. I wonder how many of them will willingly go to the hospital if other options were readily available to them. The fact that the current and previous Prime Ministers have found it necessary to go abroad for their surgeries speaks volumes by itself.*

Even if there were areas in which Mr. Raphael performed well, he is responsible for the entire health care system, and it is on his overall performance that he must be judged. To judge him otherwise is to endorse mediocrity which to my mind is totally unacceptable. Trinbagonians must demand and insist on higher standards from their elected officials otherwise Vision 2020 will remain "...but a fleeting illusion to be pursued but never attained".

When the Minister of Public Works appeared genuinely peeved and apologized for the gridlock caused by construction crews who closed off the roads in rush hour without giving prior notice to the traveling public of impending construction work, he seems unaware that people live with gridlock in T&T every day. Evidently, he too thinks that he is doing a good job and this incident is outside the norm. He seemed genuinely shocked that this piece of road caved while oblivious to the numerous potholes that punctuate the nations' roadways resulting in lost productivity, frustration, and road rage to mention a few. It wouldn't surprise me if he too feels that he should keep his job.

If you living up in Laventille for donkey years and you still don't have running water, habitable housing, social and economic investment in your community and nothing to discourage youths from gravitating to a life of crime, your government and parliamentary representatives have failed you. If anyone should ask you to give them another chance, "Ya been had! Ya been took! Ya been hoodwinked, bamboozled, led astray", according to Brother Malcolm who also said that "...all black men are not your brothers". Go figure.

This article could comment on the performance of every incumbent government minister and conclude that they leave much to be desired. This is not to say that a new constituted government will be any better or for that matter worse. Whether the incumbent government remains in power or are displaced by their rivals, it is the responsibility of the people to hold their feet to the fire and insist that they deliver on what has been false promises. In this election year vote the issues not the personalities. If current and previous politicians promised and failed to deliver before, it is unlikely that they will deliver this time around. It is only based on the issues and an insistence on quality service that T&T could move beyond mediocrity. Surely, the people of T&T deserve better.

It's Not Normal
By: Michael De Gale
Date: 6/12/2007, 10:40 am

Like the runaway crime situation, the carnage on the streets of T&T makes me wonder if anyone is in charge. Is there a ministry responsible for transportation or a police department responsible for road safety? If so, why are people being mangled daily and lives being lost unnecessarily, when tried and proven measures can be enforced to stop vehicular terrorism? How difficult is it to clamp down heavily on speedsters, inebriated and otherwise reckless drivers, street racers and all the madness that passes for driving in T&T? With the death toll more than 115 so far, these are no longer accidents; this is murder and should be prosecuted as such.

A driver's license is not a right, it's a privilege; one that should be taken away when drivers fail to exercise responsibility. The problem, however, extends beyond irresponsible drivers; the ministry of transportation and the traffic police department must also be implicated for failing to perform effectively in their respective capacities. How many families must witness the mangled remains of loved ones splattered across the nation's roadways, while curious onlookers gawk and newspaper images rob the victims of what was left of *their human dignity - prostituting journalism to create sensation and sell more newspapers? Enough already! As a society we have become too accustomed to accept mediocrity as normal. We fail to speak up and demand results from our politicians and other public officials. Consequently, anything goes even as it goes against the public's best interest.*

Ah want to tell yuh dis. It is not normal nor is it marginally acceptable, except in countries beseeched by war, for people to be slaughtered in the streets daily whether by motorized vehicles or gunfire. It is not normal nor is it acceptable for children to die in hospitals due to negligence. It may be normal, but it is not acceptable for the natural resources of any country to be exploited for the benefit of a few, when most of the population is in dire need of food, shelter and clothing. I prefer to believe that we live in a civilized society and certain things are simply not acceptable.

Regarding the carnage on the streets, I have some big ideas. How about taking away licenses, imposing stiff fines, implementing a demerit point system, jail for vehicular manslaughter and similar penalties for violating "the highway code" - if there was ever such a code? Perhaps denying insurance coverage or making premiums prohibitive for offenders will make them think twice before operating their vehicles. Oh damn! I thought that these were unique ideas; apparently these measures are routinely implemented with astounding success all over the world and are great deterrents to vehicular violence.

OK! How about this? I'm sure nobody has thought about this one before. How about holding government ministers accountable for failing to carry out their departments mandate? If they can't get the job done - FIRE THEM! Now
that's a novel idea.

Poverty - A Deadly Virus
By: Michael De Gale
Date: 5/24/2006, 9:28 am

The escalation of violent crimes in T&T has politicians, businesspeople, the police and concerned citizens not knowing which way to turn. In this climate of criminality, the Government has squandered millions in state-of-the-art technology, promised action plans which failed to materialize and most recently have invited foreign police officers to arrest the problem. At the time of this writing, the homicide rate in T&T stood at 150; 13 more murders than the number of days in the year so far. If that does not constitute a crisis, at the very lease it should provoke moral outrage. With notable exceptions, I believe that the average Trinbagonian families are "normal" people who will be content with a roof over their heads, food on the table, ample opportunities for education, employment, and social interactions. In the absence of these necessities, people will choose to live lives of quiet desperation or resort to any means necessary to ensure their own survival. Unfortunately, these things that other affluent societies take for granted are not readily available to the average citizen. Consequently, this dog-eat-dog society becomes a fertile breeding ground for pedophiles, perverts, predators, psychopaths, and thieves. This is not a prophecy as the escalation in crime indicates clearly that time is already upon us.

In desperation, people are calling on God to put a hand and stop this insanity. To gain access to the almighty they summon Benny Hinn complete with smoke, mirrors and money bags. But neither Benny Hinn, Billy Graham nor Benedict, could stem the manifestation of what is essentially a tide of social discontent, as the society continues to spiral into moral and social decay. Like Dante's Inferno, we are stuck in this living hell, a hell that is created by a government who seems incapable of responding effectively to the anguished cries of pain and suffering. Obsessed with power and saturated with pride, they are preoccupied with fighting personal battles while squandering the opportunities to create a model nation. Sadly, there is no viable opposition or emerging political party that can be expected to perform better. We are stuck between a rock and a hard place. Unlike Dante it seems that we may never emerge from this living hell. In the meantime, the most vulnerable among us must pay the price of a government's failure to order a just society for the greater good. It is the weak, the poor, and the innocent that must bear the burden of our failures. It is Akiel Chamber, Dane Andrews, baby Emily and Shawn Luke who like Jesus; would have died in vain because we failed as a society to make adequate provisions for vulnerable children.

It is shortsighted, narrow minded and cold, to believe that economic growth alone is the full measure of a prosperous society. The measure of any successful society cannot be predicated simply in terms of dollars and cents. It must by necessity factor into the equation quality of life and access to goods and services. Whether the economy doubles or triples within the next few years, if the benefits of that growth cannot be enjoyed by the lease among us, we would have essentially created a failed society. If bread and milk cannot find its way to my table at a cost that is affordable, then economic prosperity means nothing to ordinary people. If access to education, justice and social programs are not accessible to all, again economic prosperity will mean nothing. If in this land of plenty, the spoils accumulate only to a few, then I must make some decisions. In the absence of opportunities and programs that will allow me to escape this hell, I may refuse to suffer in silence, for poverty is not a natural condition. In this scenario, my hunger, anger, and frustration could conceivably place me on the other side of the law. It is easy to connect the dots and conclude that as the gap between the rich and the poor continues to widen as the economy grows, so too will the problems of violent crime, injustice, social and moral erosion.

There are many things of which the people of T&T should be proud, but poverty, crime and discrimination overshadow these accomplishments and leave an unsightly stain on the nation's fabric. As economically prosperous as the country is, the reality of life for the poor and working class makes T&T look like a banana republic. The absence of a dependable social safety net makes it difficult for the average Trinbagonian to survive economically and to feel a prolonged sense of pride. On the one hand, beggars roam the streets in naked, street children are everywhere, and citizens live in daily fear of being murdered. On the other hand, the wealthy live in grand style, flaunting their affluence for all to see, blatantly practicing racial discrimination, and robbing the country blind. The sad reality is that it does not have to be that way. Like the Government, people are becoming cold and uncaring as they battle for daily survival. Focused as they are on finding their daily bread, they fail to make the Government accountable for its actions or rather inactions. By the same token, the Government appears to have cultivated a culture of entitlement and feels itself unaccountable for mismanaging the nation's resources. Until we put in place sustainable programs to allow the lease among us to even enjoy a modicum of civility and access to opportunities, T&T will never be the paradise that it can become. Prolonged poverty is a deadly virus that stews in the cesspools of the nation and like all deadly viruses, poverty kills.

Recolonization by Invitation
By: Michael De Gale
Date: 4/5/2006, 9:06 am

"History shows that it does not matter who is in power... those who have not learned to do for themselves and have to depend solely on others never obtain any more rights or privileges in the end than they did in the beginning." -- Dr. Carter G. Woodson
Despite the outward trappings of independence, it seems that once a people are subjected to the dictates of colonialism, it is virtually impossible to break free from the inferiority complex, which that administration imposes on its subjects. Granted that the crime situation is out of control and urgent action is necessary to regain some semblance of civility in the nation, but bringing Bobbies to bust some butt is backward and bad business. If anything, it reflects poorly and speaks to the short-sightedness of past and present administrations and their colossal failure to effectively plan for the problems that often plague modern nations. Broadly speaking, it sends a negative message to the nation and more specifically, to the men and women on the T&T police force. It rips the balls right off the police commissioner and renders him effectively neutered and thoroughly emasculated. If after 43 years of independence, the best we can do is to invite Bobbies to tackle homegrown issues of law

and order, then this decision is surely indicative of a prolonged shackling of the mind. It reeks of gross incompetence within the police service and shines a revealing light on the ineptitude of the country's administration.

When T&T declared its independence from Britain on 31 August 1962, the indication was that we were going to take matters into our own hands and build our country as strong as we know how. The nation was energized by this declaration and jubilation spread throughout the land. Such a mannish maneuver rejected the popular notion that we were no more than, "hewers of wood and drawers of water". It initiated a feeling of empowerment and liberation in a people who for years, were trampled under the cruel and imperialistic boot of the Union Jack. Inviting them to come back is more than a question of law and order; it is a psychosis and is indicative of an inferiority complex. It underscores a history of vacuous leadership and historical unconsciousness.

It is not that one cannot learn from the experiences of others but the negative messages that this decision sends must be given due consideration. Independence was never a trial run; it was the real thing. It sent a clear message that we were willing to sacrifice and to plan effectively for our future, our growth and our long-term development. Evidently, we were mistaken as today, we have proven incapable of accomplishing these noble tasks for which people all over the world have fought and bled and died. We often express concern when our children emulate foreigners, but here we are imposing upon their impressionable minds, manifestations of our inferiority and confirmation of our prolonged incompetence. The vision for the future appears to be no clearer now than it was in August 1962.

If there were ever concerns about moral, racism or cultural differences within the police service, this new development can only exacerbate and add to these contentious issues. In addition to the legal implications, it also raises some fundamental but poignant questions involving race, culture, income, accommodation, authority etc. Much ado is made about Vision 2020, which increasingly appears to be predicated on more style than substance. The vision for a country must be more than the erection of tall buildings and world class stadiums. It must include an appreciation and respect for the people who live in the country. Any vision must ensure that people receive a high level of education, that there is a thriving culture and places where that culture can be placed on display, social programs for the less fortunate and a security force that serves and protects, not one that inspires fear and dread and is mired in corruption and controversy.

Since the maintenance of law and order is essential to the smooth functioning of every society, the prerequisites for entry into the police force can no longer be based on youth, strength, and ignorance. Hence, the creation of a modern police academy is fundamental to any development plan and should have been in place years ago. Such an academy would have brought some degree of respectability and professionalism to the business of policing. It would have allowed officers to take pride in their vocation and the public would have responded with respect instead of dread. Police officers should have been trained in the techniques of modern crime fighting and detection in a facility that could have been a model for neighbouring countries. Fifty million dollars would have gone a long way in turning this vision into a reality for it is said that "if you give a man a fish, you feed him for a day. If you teach him how to fish, he feeds himself for life". How much longer then, must we continue to pursue a duct tape approach to governance? In how many ways can we tell a people that they are incapable and incompetent, when it is the lack of effective leadership and a common vision that has created a social crisis and a crisis in law and order? In a country blessed with an abundance of human and natural resources, why are so many living on the fringes of society while a handful continue to horde the nation's wealth? The evidence suggests that our incapacity for long term planning and failure to create a common vision will follow us far into the foreseeable future. In that case, it may be best to surrender our sovereignty and reclaim our colonial status under the Union Jack, since we appear to be totally incapable of taking care of ourselves. We must also apologize to the queen for even entertaining the thought that we could be a sovereign nation and beg pardon for the inconvenience we may have caused the crown over the last 43 years. Perhaps she may be kind enough to allow us to drink the water with which she washed her feet, before accommodating our request to be recolonized.

Let Them Eat Bake
By: Michael De Gale
Date: 3/14/2006, 4:00 pm

Despite the lamentations and wailing, cries for relief from high food prices, protection from criminal elements, social decay and a myriad of other issues that are plaguing the country, the suffering goes unheard. However, the PNM administration had no scruples lavishing $18M on a 3-day retreat for incompetent and intellectually bankrupt ministers. This is the PNM's version of Marie Antoinette's insensitive response to cries of hunger from the French common folk. On learning that the people had no bread to eat, it is alleged that she callously responded, "Let them eat cake". In turn, she was beheaded by guillotine, the monarchy was overthrown, and the French Revolution ensued with cries of liberty, fraternity, and equality - the war cry of the French Revolution.

History is a good teacher to those who are thoughtful, reflective, and introspective. Unfortunately, the lessons of history are often lost upon the arrogant. In the presence of a laughable political opposition and no credible third party to mount a full-scale challenge for political power, the present administration is free to fritter away the country's wealth with impunity. Euripides (c480 - 406BC) informed us "those whom the Gods wish to destroy, they first make mad". It is *absolute madness to squander $18M to develop a corporation's compound for a 3-day retreat while everywhere; people are clamoring for affordable housing. I am certain that the objectives of this retreat could have been achieved in the ambiance of a less expensive resort. Since it is incomprehensible to me, why so-called "intelligent people" will make such a blatant and apparently wasteful decision, the call for transparency in Government, and the implementation of integrity legislation need to be greatly amplified and urgently implemented. In any country and by any standard, this wanton squandering of taxpayers' money is totally unacceptable.*

But the present administration knows that Trinbagonians are a people with short memories. In fact, after 40 plus years of independence, the state of politics in T&T leaves much to be desired, as people tend to believe that broken promises are just as good as the thing itself. One would think that 40 plus years is sufficient time for a nation to grow into political maturity. Instead, in the absence of innovative ideas to push the country forward, politicians continue to appeal to race - the lowest common denominator - to maintain power and divide the nation. Furthermore, there is no effective opposition to take over the reigns of government. Returning the UNC to power is to jump from the frying pan to the fire. In desperation, the hopeful cast their eyes to the heaven to pray for a political party with a common national vision. False prophets emerge from everywhere but essentially the prayers remain unanswered. In the meantime, food prices are astronomical, crime is beyond control, the masses are unsure of how much more they can bear and all the lamentations fall on deaf ears. While ministers raise their glasses to toast incompetence and loosen their pants to make room for more food, the cries of desperation go unheard. Like Marie Antoinette, the message is clear. Living high on the hog, they cannot identify with suffering and in response they say, "Let them eat cake" or more appropriately, make that "bake". Yeah! That's it. Let them eat bake.

Fete – The Opiate of the People
By: Michael De Gale
Date: 2/15/2006, 11:56 am

I want to go out on a limb here, - without the benefit of statistical data - which should but may or may not be available. I want to make a prediction that the incidences of violent crimes in T&T will hit a low point for one, perhaps two weeks after Carnival has officially ended. I am putting forward a theory; in fact, calling it a theory without some supporting evidence is stretching it. Let's just call it what it really is, a guess or better yet an educated guess which may or may not be substantiated.

I am basing this "educated guess" on the knowledge that anything that is under pressure for an extended period will explode if it finds no way to relieve itself. The presence of "safety valves" help to avert what would otherwise result in a major catastrophe. It is my contention that Carnival is such a valve. Carnival provides the opportunity for people to vent, to sing, to dance, and to release the pressure of everyday living in T&T. Carnival is the big release, the ultimate orgasm if you prefer. In fact, the series of fetes and limes that are characteristic of life in T&T are similarly, valves that reduces the build up of pressure in the society and helps to maintain the nation's sanity. These valves provide psychological relief from the stress of unemployment, lawlessness, corruption and the myriad of pressing social issues that plagues this nation state. They are valves for which the Government and the ruling class should be eternally grateful.

Never in its history has T&T experienced a period of unprecedented wealth as it is enjoying today and for the foreseeable future. As a previously colonized country and one in which people allegedly take great pride, we should seize this opportunity to build this nation as strong as we know how by investing heavily in our citizens and communities, with the natural resources that is undoubtedly making us the envy of others. It hurts my heart, when I see light shining in the heavens and darkness continues to be rolled up on one side. While some are basking in the sunshine of unfathomable wealth, too many remains mired in grinding poverty, without access to quality health care, education, housing, and other social services.

Governments are not supposed to be reactive but rather proactive. They plan not only for today, but also for future generations. In this regard, it is imperative that investments be made in communities to encourage entrepreneurship for future sustainability; in public works projects to reduce the time lost in traffic congestions and improved productivity. Invests in industries outside of oil and gas to broaden the nation's export capacity and create alternative forms of employment. Very importantly, invest in the agricultural sector to reduce the price of food and the dependence on unnecessary basic food imports. As man cannot live by bread alone, invest in culture, sports and the arts to help rescue future generations from a life of crime and similar self-destructive behaviour. Moreover, invest in people. These are some of the measures, which must be taken to build a strong and prosperous nation for the benefit of all citizens. Create a model for others to emulate. Vulgar consumption and narrow self-interest could only lead to destruction and discord. Political ambitions for self-aggrandizement must sideline itself to make way for the greater good and allow the nation's interest to take center stage.

The Canadian economist Kenneth Galbraith puts it best when he said, "...community can be as well rewarded by buying better schools and better parks as by buying bigger automobiles. It is scarcely sensible that we should satisfy our wants in private goods with reckless abundance, while in the case of public goods, we practice extreme self-denial".

I propose, that in the presence of unimaginative wealth and the absence of investments in public goods and people, it is the proliferation of the fete mentality that stops the people from making revolution. In his Critique of Hegel's Philosophy of Right, Karl Marx concluded that "religion is the opiate of the people", in T&T, I submit that the opiate fete.

Celebration All the Time
By: Michael De Gale
Date: 11/23/2005, 12:58 pm

World Cup Football, Cricket and Carnival give us insightful glimpses into the unifying possibilities that are inherent in Trinidadian society. These monumental occasions and several lesser ones are what make Trinidadians really feel like "all ah we is one.". Whether it is the euphoria, the music, the alcohol or the combined effect of all of the above, these occasions convince us that Trinidad is the greatest place on earth. Then in comes the divisive issues of politics, religion, class, and race - artificial constructs - to steal the love and make us feel that we are so fundamentally different that we can't get along on this little rock. Consequently, crime, under/unemployment, and a plethora of 'other social issues raise their ugly heads and paradise becomes a living hell.
I understand that every day cannot be World Cup, Cricket, Carnival or for that matter, any cause for celebration day, but think of the possibilities for this society if every creed and race could indeed find an equal place. No! I am not referring to Thomas Moore's Utopia. I mean T&T, A virtual paradise in the Caribbean. A model for the world to emulate. Call me naive, but I believe that this is possible. When Trinis of every stripe come together in celebration, it is not a

show but a genuine demonstration of pride and affection. For the country, as picturesque as the land may be, is nothing without the people who call it home. When I meet Trinis in the outside world, our Trinidadianess brings us together. Regardless of racial compositions or social class, that accent brings out a familiarity that warms us. The inevitable question is asked.

"You from Trinidad?"

It is as much a statement as it is a question. A knowing that is analogous to kinship.

So, what is it that creates these divisions when we are in the land we claim to love and there is no official celebration going on? We know who we are better than anyone else does. We know what we feel when we come together to celebrate on any occasion. In fact, the world stands amazed when they encounter us as individuals or as a collective. They feel our passion for life. They feel our rhythm. Yet we are not naive nor are we a stupid people. In fact, we have made and continue to make indelible marks on the pages of world history. We have competed in every arena and those who bore witness will never forget our contributions. We know these things to be true. Our artists have taken our culture throughout the world and have immortalized us in calypsos like Portrait of Trinidad, God Bless Our Nation, and If Trinidad is a Boat and other compositions. Our Carnival is now world-

renowned, and people come from everywhere to be a part of this annual celebration. We lived multiculturalism long before the word was coined. Our multiculturalism is a product of our history. The racial calaloo that are "our people" is visual evidence of this truth. According to Sniper,

"...Our scholars have sat and passed every test and put us right long side the rest".

We have made our mark in the international beauty arena. We have claimed gold in the summer Olympics. Now Soca Warriors have given us even more reason to be proud and glad. This list is not exhaustive. This little country has left a litany of indelible marks on the world stage based on our achievements in every field. All this despite only occupying an area of 1,864 square miles and a population of just over 1.3 million people. Is this not a story of biblical proportion, like that of David and Goliath or the parting of the Red Sea?

Everywhere in the world every race, every class and every religion want to carve out a piece of the earth for themselves and hug it. In their quest they practice ethnic cleansing, genocide, religious bigotry and have people dodging bullets and bombs daily. Yet, Trinidadians in this amorphous mass, find numerous common grounds for celebration. I believe in our indomitable spirit. I believe that as Trinis we could show the world how to live. Our multicultural and multi-racial makeup puts us in a unique position to be a *model nation that the rest of the world would want to emulate. We have so much to be thankful for, acres of diamonds if you will. We are rich in heritage, in resources, in talent and skill. In the deepest recesses of our Caribbean bellies, we know that our people are outstanding human beings. We have been through much together historically and we have triumphed in the face of adversity. Things that make other people cry and vouch to take revenge, we laugh it of with the knowledge that "that too shall pass" and we fire one as if it done pass already. Predictably it passes and we sit down and talk about it while having a good laugh. It is the Trinidadian way.*

Sadly, instead of rallying around the fine qualities that identify us as Trinbagonians and building upon our strengths, we gravitate towards the things that divide us as it does the rest of the world. Which Trinidadian regardless of class, colour or creed doh identify with roti, bake and shark, fete match, calypso, old talk and beach lime? Eh!

Everyday in Trinidad yuh could kill yuhself laughing just from the things that people say and do. This land is alive and pulsating. It has ah spirit that is uniquely Trinidadian but is often taken for granted. That is why we miss it so much when we are not at home. Take it from me, what we have is rare, unique and precious and must be safeguarded. The little things we take for granted is what makes life worth living. As simply as they are, these are the ties that binds us. Ah telling yuh.

Sometimes people doh really know what they have. They only miss the water after the well run dry. Doh let it come to that. Doh let politics, religion, class, and race rob us of the things that makes us who we are. Doh let Trinidad become like North America, Europe, and the rest of the world where the only thing that matters is how much money yuh have, what class yuh belong to or what is yuh race or religion. Doh let we start killing one another because we doh worship the same God. Or because we belong to different political parties. These divisive issues pit people against each other and could reap havoc in a country. They create clusters that alienate those who do not share the vision, whatever that may be. Consequently, it fuels resentment, create complexes, encourages discrimination and in worst-case scenarios, it leads to violence and bloodshed. I refuse to envision a Trinidad in which differences are denounced and colour, class, race, religion etc. are worth more than the spirit of the people who give life to this land that we claim to love.

This is not a pipe dream but a reminder that we need to be thankful for small mercies. I believe that a truly united Trinidad is possible. We have the people, we have the wealth, we have the personalities to create paradise on earth, but to do that we must ensure that things that are fundamental to minimum living standards are established. Food, housing, education, health care etc. must be rights, not privilege and must be enshrined in our constitution. Creating a society in which all people have a sense of hope and numerous opportunities for advancement, is more important than one that encourages divisions and strife. I truly believe that if we provide for the basic needs of our people, every day will bring us reasons to celebrate and the social issues that plague the country will be greatly reduced. Despite our increasing wealth, the current climate of crime, corruption, racial and political strife does not inspire hope. People are stressed, frightened, and are fleeing. Call me simplistic, naive, or ignorant, but will it really hurt to try and rescue the nation from its downward spiral? I would rather live in a land where every day brings reasons to celebrate than one in which I have no peace of mind.

For What Will it Profit...
By : Michael De Gale
Date : 10/25/2005, 3:45 pm

Gun violence in Toronto has claimed its 44th victim so far this year. In a major metropolitan city with a population of 2.48 million residents, the authorities are under tremendous pressure to address the issue with urgency. Already, businesses have expressed concern about its effect on investments and the impact on tourism. The Toronto Community Foundation released a study entitled "Vital Signs 2005", which looks at the city's economic, environmental, educational, social, and cultural health. The authors urged the Provincial Government and the public to "look beyond the headlines". The report established a link between youth violence, cuts in social programs and a feeling of alienation from the wider community among other social and economic factors. Youth (18yrs.-24yrs.) unemployment in Toronto is at a 10 year high of 17% - more than double the citywide average.

To combat the escalating violence, a "Community Safety Plan" was developed to help crime - riddled, low-income neighborhoods through a combination of tougher law enforcement and increase investment in social infrastructure. Businesses are being urged to hire young people from hard hit neighborhoods and they are responding with enthusiasm. Community *organizations have stepped up their advocacy for investment in community programs and the results are encouraging. The report asks the very pertinent question, "is it worth saving dollars by cutting social programs to end up having to later spend more on policing and the justice system?" The general response from the Government, the public and business owners is a resounding; No!*

The Toronto Dominion Bank, one of the most conservative financial institutions in Canada, recently conducted a study, which blasts the Government for reducing welfare benefits and cutting social programs. It claims that the effects of these fiscal measures have made the society more vulnerable to criminal activities and have contributed to an increase in gun violence and delinquency in the city.

By comparison, the death toll from gun violence in Trinidad has passed 300 as of September 2005 and continues to climb. The country is under siege and there appears to be no strategy to stem this disturbing tide. When asked in September if the crime situation was discussed in a ministerial meeting, Mr. Donaldson is reported to have emphatically answered, "No! We did not discuss that at all." How many more must die before the Trinidad public can see some concrete actions being taken to stem this scourge upon the land? I have always held tenaciously to the belief that worsening social conditions in certain segments of the society, widening economic disparity, a decline in quality education at the primary and secondary levels and a sense of hopelessness are major contributors to the escalating crime situation in Trinidad.

Crime is not a new phenomenon in any part of the world neither is it necessary to re-invent the wheel to address it effectively. Invariable - with notable exceptions, crime is closely associated with extenuating social problems. This creates a breeding ground for criminals and those who seek to profit from the desperation of the poor. If the crime situation is to abate, it is imperative that massive investments be made in the poorest communities. Economic development strategies, educational and social programs involving the youths, increased community law enforcement are all steps in the right direction.

In addition, it is imperative that the drugs and guns that come into the country be confiscated before they arrive at street level, and the model citizens who are involved in these trades that has the capacity to destroy societies. be prosecuted to the full extent of the law regardless of who they are.

The war on crime must take place on every level and in every community. It must involve, not just the police and the criminals but the business community and the country. How can you live in a country where you are a prisoner in your own home, afraid of being killed or kidnapped at any time of night or day? The fact is that resources and opportunities must be made available so that everyone can feel that they have a stake in the development of the country. Failure to adopt an all-inclusive strategy would only exacerbate the situation.

The Fire Next Time
By: *Michael De Gale*
Date: *9/2/2005, 4:29 pm*

From Independence to Republicanism and beyond, the people of Laventille and its environs have placed their hopes in the PNM for relieve from their long-suffering. This they demonstrated unequivocally by voting en masse to elect successive PNM administrations. To this day, they have nothing to show for their support except increasing poverty, violent communities, social stigmatization, and economic marginalization.
I can vividly recall the jubilation that radiated, particularly in these marginalized communities when the PNM won its first election in 1962. I was in the Savannah flying kite with ah set uh lil boys. Short khaki pants, sweaty, barefoot, hungry, and half-naked - descendants of the third estate of colour. I was about 8 years old at the time and as my mother would often say, "we like to drivay." In the distance, we see ah ban comin rong the savannah, beating drum, ringin iron and singing "when PNM go marching home." Although we did not know it at the time, this was a celebration of hope, a celebration of promise. In retrospect, they were giving thanks in song for relief from years of neo-colonial exploitation. Massa day was finally over for those that Fanon called "the wretched of the earth." It was liberation time and our destiny lay in the palm of

our hands. Without a second thought, we aiyo the kites, jump in de ban and shake we bony ass all the way home. The celebration lasted deep into the wee hours of the morning until people retreated to their homes in the cracks and crevices of Belmont, the broken-down buildings behind the bridge and the shacks balancing delicately on the hills of Laventille. Better days were coming they believed, but time dashed hopes and visions faded as that day never came. It was as if they miss the bus. Everybody else could see his or her way. Even foreigners found prosperity while these communities continue to wrestle with poverty and its accompanying manifestations. Amazingly, after 43 years of independence, the PNM could still count on support from those improvised community where some continue to cherish the hope that things will get better. After all, that is the promise that is made every election, when wolves in sheep clothing come begging for votes hoping to assume power without taking responsibility for the alleviation of human suffering. Independence may have brought a new administration but is the same old khaki pants.

Deprived of innovative programs, which would enable them to improve themselves and develop their communities, these people are systematically relegated to the bottom rungs of the social and economic ladders. Access to capital for economic development is impossible to secure through traditional *financial institutions. Post secondary education to liberate mind and body is still reserved for the independently wealthy and social programs to ease the strain leaves much to be desired. DEWD, URP and more recently CPEP - the crumbs from the economic table - is used as bait to satisfy short-term hunger, ensure re-election but holds no promise of sustainable development.*

Prophetically, old people say that "ingratitude is worst than obeah." It is no surprising then, that criminal activities emanating from these historically neglected communities are reaching pandemic proportions. The seeds of discontent were planted decades ago and nurtured for generations by successive PNM administrations. Governments, who failed to implement mechanisms to empower the members of these communities to ensure sustainable growth and development. Instead, they are used as pawns in an elaborate scheme to assume power and maintain the status quo.

In his book, "The Dragon Can't Dance", Earl Lovelace captured the essence of the people of these communities. He revealed their hopes, their dreams, their aspirations and showed that theirs are fundamentally like all human beings. The need for food, shelter, and opportunities to secure a better life is central to the human condition. We read this book, shared their pain and vicariously experienced their hunger. We know Philo and Fisheye and Aldrick and Sylvia and Guy. We know Miss Olive, Miss Cleotilda, Miss Caroline and all her hungry children. We know them because they are, in all their colourful manifestations, the proud people of Trinidad and Tobago. Despite the variations in colour and class distinctions, they have contributed greatly to the economy, culture, history and more importantly, to the formation of the Trinidadian personality. No world-renowned pannist, calypsonian or limbo dancer ever originated from Goodwood Park, Federation Park or Elleslie Park as far as I am aware. These are only the consumers of this rich heritage, which allows them to say with pride that they are Trinis. Marginalized Trinidadians created the compass that allows people to locate us on the map of human geography. Yet, they are the cousins of whom we are painfully ashamed and treat with utter disregard.

Like Haiti, we immortalize them in song but fail to render concrete support to enable them to elevate themselves and take their rightful, productive place in the society. They have been mired in poverty for so long, despite the country's unimaginable wealth that poverty appears to be a normal condition. The people of Laventille and surrounding areas are vibrant, energetic and enterprising. When water is more than flour, they make bread out of stone. We see them ply their trade on the streets of Port of Spain. They give life to Carnival, Emancipation, and similar cultural celebrations. They infuse a natural energy into the society by virtue of their determination to live out loud. It is only their sheer determination to survive that keeps them from being torn asunder.

According to David Rudder, out of this muddy pond 10,000 flowers bloomed. However, this represents only a small fraction of the human potential currently beseeched by crime, drugs, and other poverty- related problems that are consuming these communities. I do not know what strange celestial bodies; preparation and opportunity may have aligned to liberate some from this smoldering cauldron, but sustained and deliberate efforts would do much to liberate future generations. Grinding poverty is not a natural condition nor is it a curse for being the children of Ham. This poverty was meticulously orchestrated historically and structurally interwoven into the very fabric of the nation.

The culture of crime that is currently plaguing the country will not go away overnight neither will it be permanently eliminated by increasing the number of police and military personnel. These are only stopgap measures to protect private property, safeguard the wealthy but do nothing to address the root causes of social deviance. Decades of economic neglect, failure to provide opportunities for community development and empowerment, limited access to post secondary education are only some of the issues that need to be addressed. We callously accept that life for people in depressed areas is a normal phenomenon and hence socially acceptable. They live on the periphery of society and every effort is made to ensure that they never gravitate from margin to center. By sheer neglect, they are blatantly denied their humanity and consequently are not deserving of human consideration. The constant shortage of water, no electricity, and other necessities of life that others take for granted are denied them decade after decade. How much longer must this go on? The Government must demonstrate substantively, a serious commitment to improving the conditions of existence in these areas. Crime will not go away for the long term by simply increasing police presence. Every day a new batch of children are born in a country in which they do not share in the wealth. With notable exceptions, people are not born criminals, dire circumstances; illiteracy and desperation are major ingredients in the making of the criminal mind. Storm clouds are gathering in the form of desperate young people with nothing to lose, in a nation in which they are increasingly and systematically alienated. We will eat the bread that the devil kneads, if we fail to act decisively to include those who live on the margins of society in the developmental process. Or, to quote James Baldwin – "The fire next time."

Where have all the Good Men Gone?
By: Michael De Gale
Date: 7/27/2005, 8:33 am

Where have all the good men gone? The Caribbean visionaries who advocated for a united Caribbean stretching from the Bahamas in the north to Surinam in the south. From Central America in the west to Barbados in the east. Men who envisioned a Caribbean where trade and economic corporation flows as easily as the tides that wash these blessed shores. Where are the men who knew instinctively that Caribbean unity is fundamental to the region's survival in the global economy? Men, who before the discovery of oil and natural gas, the mortar that can hold the region together, advocated the need for Caribbean solidarity to stave off marginalization, economic dependency and exploitation, Men who believed, that a common history and culture were ties, strong enough to foster Caribbean unity and economic empowerment? Men who knew that it is folly to sit back and react to global developments rather than adopt a proactive approach. Where are the likes of Shiradat Ramphal, Dr. Eric Williams, Marcus Garvey, Bob Marley, Dr. Cheddi Jagan, Arthur Lewis and Michael Manley from the English-speaking Caribbean? Where is Fidel Castro, Roberto Fernandez Retamar and Jose

Marti our Spanish speaking brethren's? Where are Aime Cesaire, Frantz Fanon and Antenor Firmin of the French Caribbean islands? Men of vision and substance who understood that the whole is greater than the sum of its parts. I could name dozens more men and women from every area of the Caribbean who saw the infinite wisdom of a united Caribbean region, but for now perhaps someone can tell me, where have all the good men gone?

We stand by and watch helplessly as Haiti, the breadbasket of France and its most profitable possession in the 16th century disintegrate into a cesspool of poverty and all we could say is "Haiti I'm sorry." Haiti demonstrated convincingly that we are more than chattel by defeating the French and establishing the first black republic in history. Today, Haiti is less than a shadow of its former self. How much longer must Haiti suffer for casting off the chains of slavery and establishing itself as an independent republic and a model for African liberation?

Cuba is another Caribbean country under economic siege for over 45 years for resisting the exploitation of its people and its resources. Despite its extenuating economic circumstances, Cuba continues to lend its technical expertise to Caribbean, Latin American and Africa countries. Economic co-operation with Cuba would create a model to show that another economic arrangement is indeed possible. By contrast, the US exports death, destruction and economic dependency as a developmental strategy while filling its coffers with other people's money. The Caribbean Basin including Venezuela, Columbia and Central America represents a community more than 112 million. Include Mexico and we are up to 200 million. Establish trading links with Africa and India and the number become staggering. Considering all these possibilities, where are the visionaries who could turn this dream into a reality? Instead, we allow the US to dictate with whom we should become friendly. We stand by and allow them to remove any number of democratically elected presidents from office and replace them with imperialist stooges. If all these things do not underscore the need for creating stronger ties with fellow nations, I do not know what would.

Hugo Chavez in Venezuela has proposed Petrocaribe, the Energy Co-operation Agreement. This is a proposal we need to consider seriously and not summarily dismiss because the US opposes it. In fact, US opposition is usually a damn good sign that something is good for a people. This could be the beginning of an emerging Third World, economically powerful and financially viable. Venezuela provides 5% of the world's oil and Trinidad is said to be awash in oil and natural gas for decades to come. These are excellent building blocks for the establishment of a strong Caribbean economy. Disagreement about the feasibility of the Petrocaribe proposal represents an opportunity to fine tune the agreement, not a reason for its disintegration. The disagreement that resulted in the failure of the proposed that caused dr. Williams to proclaim that 10-1= 0 must never be repeated. Petty differences must not stand in the way of corporation and development of the Caribbean region. If the US could cozy up to China and Russia despite their communist history and ongoing allegations of human rights abuses, relations with other Caribbean nations including Cuba, Venezuela and Haiti is indeed possible and should be vigorously encouraged.

Trinidad and Venezuela are the Saudi Arabia of the Caribbean. After three decades of intense modernization, Saudi Arabia transformed itself into a modern nation providing the best in medical, educational, and social services to its people. Despite its relatively small geographic area and a population of approximately 1.5 million people, it is one of the world's biggest power brokers. Its development was strategic and goal oriented. After inviting foreign companies to develop its oil facilities and making scholarships and various strategic opportunities available to its citizens, Saudi Arabia now controls the lion's share of its economy including oil production and distribution. There is a lesson here. Let us learn it well.

The creation of a Caribbean trading block encompassing South and Central America with links to

India and Africa is visionary and a monumental proposition. It offers numerous challenges as well as tremendous opportunities for growth and development. It requires men and women of vision and substance. Who will heed this clarion call? Must we forever kowtow to US imperialism and be treated like the illegitimate children of the global economy? Must we always seek handouts in times of trouble and foreign aid designed to separate us from our wealth and human dignity? Though they have beaten us for hundreds of years, I assure you that we have the strength of millions. Let us stand up in our countless numbers, united by history, hope and a dogged determination to "build our castles as strong as we know how." Failing to do so is a clear indication that all the good men are gone.

Courting Disaster – Racism, Rhetoric & Regression
By: *Michael De Gale*
Date: *5/18/2005, 9:10 am*

The proliferation of race talk in Trinidad is indicative of a crumbling society, despite its unprecedented economic growth, continues to freefall into social decline. By scraping the bottom of the barrel respected members of society embrace racism, nationalism, class differentiation and religious differences to rally support for their self-serving agenda. The fragmentation of society based on race, class religion etc. leaves in its trail horrific memories of the Jewish Holocaust, Bosnia, India, Rwanda and closer to home, Guyana in the 1960's to mention just a few. In the end lives are destroyed and the painful pieces are difficult to put together again. The promulgation of social division based on race is a sure sign that a nation has lost its way. Evidently, the lessons of history have been lost upon us.
Dr. Elizabeth Sieusarran was the latest to wade into the cesspool of racist rhetoric (Trinidad Express 16/05/05). Her thinly veiled attempt to cover up her message of hate was pathetic to say the least. Who are these Dougla people to whom she is referring? Are they a sub cast like the untouchables in her ancestral India? What does she mean by "...do we accept them or ostracize them?" Does she envision herself as a

member of a superior race? Is Trinidad and Tobago the patrimony of the East Indians more so than the Africans who laboured for free and by force for hundreds of years prior to the arrival of East Indians as indentured servants? What about the other races who have been here for what seems like forever? Are they all not people with hopes and dreams like she and her cabal? I have no qualms with people taking pride in and embracing their heritage but not at the expense of others. Trinidad is a multi-cultural/ethnic society and racial intermarriage; religious and cultural influences are to be expected. Isolation is not an option for a multi-cultural/ religious/ ethnic society anywhere in the modern world. It is regressive, divisive and potentially explosive. It is isolation that ushered in Europe's "Dark Ages" which lasted for almost 500 years.

The selling off valuable land to foreigners is a greater national issue than the racial flames she is fanning. Increasing poverty in this cornucopia, the lack of social programs, the lack of accountability by Government Ministries, drugs, corruption, sensationalism in the media, street children, education, affordable housing policies are all issues to which she can direct her energy and intellect. It is not for lack of important social issues that she has chosen to stoop to the lowest common and divisive denominator. Rather, it is her tribal instinct and false notions of assumed superiority which blinds her from embracing a common humanity.

Her refusal to accept others who appear to be different, diminishes her and brings into question her intellectual achievements. In unity there is strength, growth, and promise. Show love, give people hope and society will flourish. Do not extinguish the flame of ambition in the heart of youths, forcing them to gravitate to criminal activity as a viable alternative to education because of their ethnicity. When this happens, no one could be safe even in gated communities. The legacy of colonialism with its exploitation of racial difference must no longer be tolerated. It is past time that the artificial construct of race be relegated to the dustbin of history. Contemporary scientific evidence dispels old notions of racial superiority. Racism has no place in a progressive society. Being an educator, her job is to build not to destroy. If she must emulate other, may I suggest she take her cue from more enlightened and progressive nations?

Canada is perhaps the most successful example in North America of what it means to live in a multicultural society. It is still a work in progress but already it is paying huge dividends in terms of peaceful co-existence in addition to numerous tangible benefits. All things considered; Canada is a model nation. When Canada adopted its official policy of multiculturalism July 21, 1988 during the Trudeau era, it was met with varying degrees of resistance. Since then, the policies and practices have become entrenched, creating a more harmonious, productive, civil society. It is a strong nation in which differences are respected and similarities are celebrated. It is a good and decent society in which to live. A model nation rich with diversity, respected throughout the world, inclusive and prosperous.

Anti-discrimination laws must be implemented NOW and vigorously enforced if Trinidad is to avoid the inevitable bloodbath that accompanies irresponsible spew. It is not a matter of freedom of speech; it is a matter of responsible utterances. The word is indeed mightier than the sword but more frighteningly, it has the capacity to cause the sword to be drawn. The realization of Vision 2020 with its aspiration to achieve first world status, necessitate that people be held accountable for their words as well as their deeds. Implement and vigorously enforce progressive laws for the greater good. Let the nation know that tribalism will not be tolerated. No society can exist in a vacuum especially in the face of increasing globalization. More so, the fragmentation of a society based on race is not a formula for success; it is a recipe for disaster and ultimately, obliteration.

In essence, for what will it profit a nation, if it gains the whole world and suffer the loss of its freedom and internal security to escalating crime and increasing violence?

The Vampire Mentality of MNCs
By: *Michael De Gale*
Date: *3/7/2005, 1:56 pm*

Couva South MP Kelvin Ramnath's condemnation of the Government's move to renew the privilege of multinational oil and gas companies involved in offshore exploration is well founded and should be vigorously supported. It is common knowledge that Multinational Corporations (MNCs), particularly those involved in the energy sector, suck more than oil and gas from the host countries, they suck the very spirit and the lifeblood of working people. Except for a handful of individuals, every "Third World" country in which MNC's operate are left more improvised and environmentally devastated than before their arrival. In his continuing struggle to make Shell accountable for the grinding poverty of the Ogoni people in Nigeria - despite their tremendous oil wealth - and the destruction of their environment among other issues, activist/writer Ken Saro- Wiwa, stated from his prison cell: "My lord, we all stand before history. I am a man of peace, of ideas. Appalled by the denigrating poverty of my people who live on a richly endowed land, distressed by their political marginalization and economic strangulation, angered by the devastation of their land, their ultimate heritage, anxious to preserve their right to life and to a decent living, and determined to usher to this country as a whole a fair and just democratic system which protects everyone and every ethnic group and gives us all a valid claim to human civilization, I *have devoted my intellectual and material resources, my very life, to a cause in which I have total belief and from which I cannot be blackmailed or intimidated. I have no doubt at all about the ultimate success of my cause, no matter the trials and tribulations which I and those who believe with me may encounter on our journey. Nor imprisonment nor death can stop our ultimate victory. "*

Despite the justice of his cause and his reasonable demands, writer/activist Ken Saro-Wiwa and eight other Ogoni activists were hanged in Port Harcourt, Nigeria on November 10, 1995 by the Nigerian military government in collaboration with Shell. This, unfortunately is not an isolated case. There is no shortage of examples globally, in which MNCs take more than they give and leave behind environmental devastation, corruption and death. Soudan and Bhopal immediately come to mind. The questions are: how do Trinbagonians avoid a similar fate? How do we ensure that the natural resources of our country are exploited for the benefit of all our citizens and not just the oil and gas companies and a handful of local elites? The answers lie in the adage which says, "if you give a man a fish you feed him for a day. If you teach him how to fish you feed him for life." The fact is that Trinidad has been a petroleum producing country for far too long to continue to depend of foreign companies to develop our oil and gas resources. The royalties that oil and gas companies pay the government to extract our resources is pocket change when compared to the profits they make from gas, oil and its byproducts. But we don't need a light to see the sun. What we need is vision to see the future. Our continued dependence on foreign expertise would always leave us vulnerable. We will always have to make compromising arrangements with MNCs in the forms of tax moratoriums and duty-free concessions. Since oil and gas does not spoil and the reserves are estimated to last far into the future, it is not too late to put in place the necessary mechanisms which would allow us to control and develop these resources. In the meantime, we should try and drive a harder bargain, as greater income is essential to the realization our long-term goal. Demanding transparency between the government and MNCs a reasonable as these resources belong to the people of T&T. Transparency would ensure that we get value for our resources. If anything, history has taught us that we must look after our own best interest.

I do not know if Vision 2020 includes the ownership and development of the energy sector. If it doesn't, it's terribly flawed and desperately in need of tweaking with oil and gas. This is the most lucrative part of our economy; we must take charge of all aspects of it for future prosperity. Failure to do so could sentence countless future generations to a lifetime of weeping and gnashing of teeth. Mr. Ramnath, as Black Stalin suggested, "keep the fire burning vampires passing." Yours is a righteous cause for the greater good.

Miseducation, Identity & Mischief
By: Michael De Gale
Date: 11/24/2004, 2:38 pm

In a letter to the editor of the Trinidad Guardian entitled "Wrong to call them Africans" 27/10/04, Dr. Chris Mahadeo referred to PhD friends of his from various countries in Africa who take umbrage with being called Africans. Emphasizing the intellectual accomplishments of his friends, the good doctor went on to denounce Afro-Trinidadians for referring to their African heritage when identifying themselves. The argument being, that if these highly educated people born in Africa, don't identify themselves as Africans, why should Afro-Trinidadians feel compelled to make this connection? The answer can be found in a book entitled "The Mis-education of the Negro" by Carter G. Woodson, here, Woodson spoke of the attitude of contempt that the "educated Negro" have toward his own people. "He is taught to admire the Hebrews, Greeks, Latin et al and to despise the African.". Add Dr. Morgan Job to Dr. Mahadeo's Not-African-African PhD friends and nuff said.

Whether we like it or not, identity plays an integral role in helping us to understand who we are as a people in the diaspora. Every ethnic group understands that they must know from whence and from whom they came. This is their source of strength. The knowledge of their history empowers them and provides the foundation they require to make positive contributions wherever they are throughout the Diaspora.

Unfortunately, the history of slavery and colonisation has had a devastatingly negative effect on African people. Consequently, today we continue to struggle to re-establish our roots by embracing our African heritage. By contrast, the Chinese, Indians, Europeans, Hispanics etc. by virtue of their names and physical appearance alone are automatically associated with a continuous history, a culture and geographic locations. They have foundations upon which they can build. These foundations, we too need to establish and upon them we can build our castles as tall as we know how. I ask Dr. Mahadeo therefore, not to denigrate the black man for identifying himself with his African heritage. As you very well know, American law once classified black people as chattel and anyone with one ounce of black blood in their veins was considered black. After years of being made to feel ashamed of our African selves, we now embrace this self to the fullest. We gladly accept that definition because we know of Africa's rich history. This awareness gives us courage and the dignity to project ourselves into the future with assurance and hope. It gives us the will, to perform honourably in the pageant of mankind. We no longer believe "his-story" about Africans making no contribution to the development of civilisation. We know that Africans gave civilisation to the world as one of her numerous and thankless contributions. We know and embrace "our-story". Perhaps his friends are still reading "his-story" and continue to deprecate themselves and their African heritage. For your mis-educated non-African friends born in Africa Dr. Mahadeo, allow me to once again quote Carter G. Woodson:

"When you control a man's thinking you do not have to worry about his actions. You do not have to tell him not to stand here or go yonder. He will find his "proper place" and will stay in it. You do not need to send him to the back door. He will go without being told. In fact, if there is no door, he will cut one for his special benefit. His education makes it necessary."

Although this book was first published in 1933, prevailing evidence as the doctor have presented suggests, that it is as relevant today as it was back then. If Dr. Mahadeo's non-African-African PhD friends are typical of educated Africans in Africa, this may add to our understanding of the turmoil in various countries on the continent particularly the ones from which his friends originated. On the other hand, perhaps this is Dr. Mahadeo's subtle contribution to the increasing racial tension between African and Indian Trinidadians - another salvo on the broadside to sink the ship of African consciousness or to derail the train of Pam-Africanism. Whatever the objective may be, I found his letter to be offensive and objectionable. His Indian heritage has never been questioned in Trinidad or in any part of the world for that matter. I feel assured that he has never had occasion to correct anyone for calling him an Indian. Despite the presence of Indians in Trinidad for generations, they still derive great pride from their illustrious East Indian heritage. If the good doctor does not, he should. In our efforts to identify ourselves with our African heritage, please be respectful of us as we are of you. If you must comment on the issue of identity, may I suggest you keep it within your community. Such condescending comments by *people like yourself could only fan the flames of racial intolerance in the country you referred to as "sweet Trinidad". Let's try to keep it that way.*

Conclusion

The articles were born out of frustration and predominantly addressed the pressing social and political issues affecting the nation, devoid of any partisan agenda. While they garnered widespread acclaim, I ultimately questioned their efficacy and opted to discontinue the pursuit.

Having spent over three decades in Canada, I have since developed a profound sense of belonging here. Though the initial sense of loss upon leaving Trinidad has diminished, yet a lingering attachment to the island remains. Despite only infrequent visits back, I do not fit the stereotype of an immigrant torn between two worlds. Neither does my embrace of Canada signify a lack of concern for Trinidad; rather, I am deeply troubled by the persistent socio-political and economic challenges plaguing my homeland.

As I approach another year's end, thoughts of the sunny island persist, contrasting with the wintry realities I now face. Recollections of its natural beauty and cultural richness evoke nostalgia, tempered by the stark changes witnessed over time. While Trinidad holds allure, the prospect of returning and effecting change at this point in my life feels daunting. Trinidad and Tobago, with its vibrancy and potential, remains close to my heart. Yet, the dream of reliving its festivities is juxtaposed with a sober acknowledgment of its ongoing struggles. Despite this, my enduring residence in Canada, where generations of my family have thrived, reaffirms my commitment to this adopted home. While nostalgia may tinge my reflections, my roots are now firmly planted in Canadian soil, even as distant echoes of Trinidad's allure persist through the Call of the Cascadura.

www.ingramcontent.com/pod-product-compliance
Lightning Source LLC
Chambersburg PA
CBHW071221080526
44587CB00013BA/1454